A CHURCHLESS FAITH

Alan Jamieson is a minister who has also trained as a sociologist. His PhD, on which this book is based, researched why people leave their churches and their journeys of faith outside the church.

From this study, he and others at Wellington Central Baptist Church, New Zealand, have created resources for individuals who leave church, and are developing resources for churches to help them respond to and care for those who leave.

D0113352

A Churchless Faith

Faith journeys beyond the churches

Alan Jamieson

Published in Great Britain in 2002 by
Society for Promoting Christian Knowledge
Holy Trinity Church
Marylebone Road
London NW1 4DU

First published in New Zealand in 2000 by Philip Garside Publishing Ltd

British Library Cataloguing-in-Publication Data

A catalogue record for this book is available from the British Library

ISBN 0–281–05465–7

Typeset by Wilmaset Ltd, Birkenhead, Wirral
Printed in Great Britain by
The Cromwell Press Ltd, Trowbridge, Wiltshire

Acknowledgements

Grateful thanks to Dr Bob Hall and Professor David Thorns (of the Sociology Department at Canterbury University, New Zealand), who supervised my research, and to Jenny McIntosh, who has worked with me to create and develop Spirited Exchanges.

Contents

Foreword   ix

1   Face to face with those who leave   1
2   EPC churches   19
3   The leaving process   29
4   Disillusioned followers   46
5   Reflective exiles   60
6   Transitional explorers   75
7   Integrated wayfinders   91
8   Bringing it all together . . . where's the map?   106
9   Jumping ship – making your own way   126
10 Leaver-sensitive churches   141
11 Searching for a place to belong   152

Bibliography   172
Index   177

Foreword

The book you hold in your hands addresses a set of challenges that face more and more persons of faith, and their churches, in the twenty-first century. Its author knows the terrain he describes from personal experience, professional responsibility and academic research. Alan Jamieson, pastor and scholar, uses personal interviews, his work with groups and his research to help us understand how people may outgrow the patterns of faith offered in their churches. He studies how members who are drawn to the fellowship of evangelical and Pentecostal churches may find that for their faith to grow, they have to experience struggle and doubt, and in some cases, form or find new communities of faith.

Dr Jamieson is a pioneer in the use of faith development theory and research. He illumines how pastoral care and spiritual direction – for persons and for groups – can help people make necessary transitions in their stage of faith for the sake of being faithful to Christ.

You will find in Alan Jamieson an excellent writer, a trustworthy interpreter of theory and research, and a compassionate counsellor and pastor. He offers a book both scholarly and practical. It stays close to human experience. It brings a compassionate spirit to the task of understanding the dynamics of growth and change in faith.

Written for professional researchers and pastoral leaders, Jamieson's book is also accessible to thoughtful laypersons who want to study alone or together to better understand and grow in their faith journeys. I commend the book and its author to you with confidence and appreciation.

JAMES W. FOWLER

Candler Professor of Theology and Human
Development, Emory University, Atlanta, USA

Author of *Stages of Faith: The Psychology of
Development and the Quest for Meaning*

ONE

Face to face with those who leave

I used to go with the multitude,
leading the procession to the house of God,
with shouts of joy and thanksgiving
among the festive throng.
Why are you downcast, O my soul?
Why so disturbed within me?

Psalm 42:4–5

Introduction

Every now and then our understandings of 'how things are' get jolted by a reality that we would never have foreseen and could not have anticipated. Our paradigms are forced to change. Our perceptions are altered. An unnerving experience of this kind began for me the evening I met the first church leavers I would formally interview. My notes of that evening in August 1993 record being met by a tall slim man in his mid-thirties, who introduced himself as Stuart as he warmly invited me into his home. While walking through to the lounge Stuart talked of how he and his wife, Michelle, were very interested in the research I was doing. In fact they had been eagerly looking forward to tonight so they could talk about it with me. As he offered to make a cup of coffee Stuart explained that Michelle was finishing reading a bedtime story to their two young children and would be out to join us soon. Stuart, a medical doctor, then began to explain that since leaving their Pentecostal church five years ago they had been involved in a small group of people who had also left similar churches. That evening Stuart and Michelle introduced me to the complex web of involvements they had with the Christian church, their reasons for eventually leaving and the ongoing nature of their Christian faith.

1

As I approached their driveway I thought I knew what happened to the Christian faith of those who left the church. I'd seen others leave the growing charismatic church where I was a pastor and I'd read about church leavers. Walking back down Stuart and Michelle's drive two and a half hours later I was bewildered. This couple just didn't fit my expectations. They had left their leadership roles in a growing Pentecostal church five years before I came to meet them, yet during their time outside the church their faith had obviously continued to develop, their understanding of God at work in their lives was undoubtedly continuing. They were also involved in their community as part of the outworking of their faith. Contrary to my impression of church leavers, Stuart and Michelle had been leaders within their church and well respected within the Christian community in Woking. They were young parents who were obviously very concerned about the faith of their children. They had been brought up within the Christian church from childhood and there was no obvious evidence of a crisis in their own lives or the life of the church that had precipitated their leaving. As I was later to establish, Stuart and Michelle were not an exceptional case but part of a steady stream of people who were leaving churches like theirs when they felt they could no longer stay and continue to develop in their Christian faith.

During our conversation that evening Michelle told me she had been brought up as an Anglican and was, as she said, 'well churched'. By this comment she was summing up the very strong commitment her family had to their church during her childhood and teenage years. However, this had not prepared her for her own conversion experience in her mid-teens. As Michelle said, 'When I made a personal response at secondary school it was an extraordinary and challenging and all-encompassing thing for me. It was a very emotional time. I received the Holy Spirit, which I knew nothing about. It was a total culture shock but the reality of it was very much embedded in me and I could just see that this was very real.'

For Michelle, this was the beginning of a 14-year involvement in both para-church[1] groups and a Pentecostal church. During this time she was involved as a worship leader, children's work leader, youth group leader and later on supporting her husband as an elder in the church.

Stuart, like Michelle, had some association with the church as he was growing up. His mother sent him to the local Presbyterian church at least once a fortnight for 'at least four years'. Stuart remembers these times in church as 'boring and irrelevant', something which was quite different from his own experience of God in his late teenage years in the Pentecostal church he chose to join when he was 17. Particularly he remembers being confronted by God through a popular Christian book – *The Cross and the Switchblade* – that was doing the rounds in the 1970s. Through the life of David Wilkerson, the author and central character of the book, Stuart saw a God 'who actually does something'. As the book outlined the journey of this young American minister to the ghettoes of New York to try and help young people caught in gangs, crime and drugs, Stuart's sense of God at work grew. The miraculous conversion of Nicky Cruz and other gang members 'made an enormous impact' on Stuart, who for the first time seemed to be reading about the 'real thing'.

From this personal and very real encounter with God Stuart became a strongly committed Christian, a leader within the young people's group at his church and involved in youth work in the city. Not long after becoming a Christian he moved from the church he had been attending (because of his mother's insistence) to a growing Pentecostal church with a large group of young adults. Eventually Stuart became an elder of this church for a number of years before co-founding a suburban branch in their own area of Woking. In the new church he was committed to leading as an elder, regular preacher and leader of home groups right up to the time he and Michelle chose to leave.

Central figures in the life of their own church, Stuart and Michelle were also involved in a number of Christian organizations around the city and were seen as respected leaders within the Christian community. Yet they decided to leave the church they had helped establish and lead. In choosing to leave they were not moving to another church but leaving church altogether. Their decision was not because of leadership struggles within the church, although leadership issues were a factor. Nor was it a rejection of their Christian faith, although there were doubts and questions regarding certain aspects of 'faith' that were presented in their church. It was not because of personal difficulties with people in the church nor was it a result of a desire to pursue new leisure or work opportunities that conflicted with church time. On the contrary, Stuart and Michelle were to

3

be instrumental in the formation of a group for church leavers which would regularly meet in their home for the next five years.

Unravelling the reasons for their decision to leave the church revealed the multiple interconnected factors and influences involved. For Michelle these were a mixture of:

> *Michelle* . . . power issues, women's issues and some of my own stuff . . . my need to please, to perform highly, function highly. Many of these issues were dealt with in therapy. But it started the ball rolling in my mind and I found that I was living with a tension which became increasingly unbearable. I tried very hard to smooth it over, plaster over, wallpaper over it. I tried ways of getting round it by being more honest from the pulpit, going against the system and using language which was everyday language rather than religious language. I tried to model what I thought was really real and honest for me and once again I found that I really had no peers in the church, no one who said, 'Hey, I really feel like that too.' People would say it to me privately, but I didn't have a friend or a close soulmate who I felt was going the same place as me. I became involved in leadership and I found that even then, when I was fairly important within the church, I was still fairly unlistened to. Listened to but not heard.

The personal issues that Michelle described were a combination of her own mild depression and the grief and struggle of living with the severe health problems of their children. For Stuart, in contrast, the issues took on a more intellectual and structural focus; concerns about the lack of connection between church and work environments and the general life experience of so many people, what he called the 'sacred–secular split'. He also perceived a lack of space within the church for the kinds of questions that educated or intellectual people might bring. Over a period of time Stuart said that he began to feel that he too no longer fitted.

> *Stuart* Eventually for me I was kind of valued as someone who was coming from a different perspective and had provoking, challenging things to say. When we started up Ashforth Free Church,[2] I and a couple of the others were mainly responsible for the preaching, which was a useful outlet for doing something to change the system. But I increasingly came to see that people were where they were at, and I was where I was at and it wasn't necessary for them to follow the same path that I was following, to ask the questions I was asking. But I was never going to be satisfied within that

sort of framework, not that I was really actually looking for satisfaction, but it just came to a point where it was pointless to continue on with it.

And so Stuart and Michelle began to feel that their involvement in the church was no longer rewarding. These factors on their own would probably not have led them to leave the church. They had seen too many others do that, many of whom were close friends, and didn't want to leave amid the tension and conflict these friends had. This desire was bolstered by what Michelle called their 'tremendously loyal streak'.

In the end, two unrelated factors helped these loyal, long-term leaders of the church to finally come to their decision. The first was the fact that the church they had helped to pioneer was going well, had a new pastor and they were no longer needed to the same degree as they had been previously. Second they had met up with two other married couples of similar age who also had been very involved in long-term Christian leadership and had the same feelings of dissatisfaction with the church.[3] Although these couples went to different churches they expressed similar feelings of no longer fitting within their churches. These couples were also strongly committed to their Christian faith and had each spent several years in full-time leadership roles within an evangelistic para-church organization. Alongside this para-church work they were also involved in their churches but to a lesser extent than Stuart and Michelle had been.

For over a year the three couples met together and talked about their growing dissatisfaction with church and their desire to find a group of Christians with whom they could meet and discuss things in new ways. In the end it was to be the setting up of this new small group of people with similar journeys and concerns that provided the impetus for Stuart and Michelle to leave. Once begun, the group quickly grew from three couples to 12 to 15 people. Interestingly, although the group was to be highly significant for all the church leavers it attracted, none of the group members I met considered the group as church.

Although Stuart and Michelle's Christian faith has changed since leaving the church they were quick to acknowledge the reality of their previous experience of God in the church. As Stuart said:

Stuart I had experiences in the past, transcendent experiences where I have absolutely no doubt whatsoever that God has been involved in my life and

5

done certain things. And he's actually moved in and broken into the here and now, time and space as something from outside my life. There is no doubt. I shouldn't say there is no doubt, but there is no real doubt that God exists and that he is real and cares and is concerned about me and everyone else.

Can we understand Stuart and Michelle and church leavers like them? Is there an underlying logic to their decision to leave? Can the mix of personal, church and faith issues that they spoke of be brought together in some coherent way? Does the journey of these leavers offer hope and something of a map for other church leavers wanting to continue a Christian faith outside their previous churches? Equally, can an understanding of their leaving and their faith journey outside the church help church leaderships and ministers in their role with other potential leavers in the future? And finally, does their leave-taking give us clues to the shape of emerging communities of faith (churches) in an increasingly postmodern culture? I believe the answer to all these questions is yes! This book sets out to answer these questions. However, before we move to analyse each of these significant concerns, let me explain the basis for the answers.

The present study

The comments presented here are based on research that has spanned the last six years and been my predominant area of reading and reflection throughout this time. It encapsulates information brought together through a number of unique sources. Stuart and Michelle are two of the 108 church leavers interviewed for a doctoral thesis in sociology, on faith outside the Christian church. This thesis, which also incorporates 54 interviews with church leaders, focuses on those who leave evangelical, Pentecostal and charismatic churches, and their post-church faith journeys. At the time of submission (January 1998) this was, and remains to my knowledge, the most extensive qualitative research on the faith of church leavers from the evangelical, Pentecostal and charismatic streams of the church.

In addition to the thesis research base are the accounts of many other church leavers. These include contributions that might be described as anecdotal but nevertheless added to the depth of understanding on which this study is based. They include people who responded to magazine and newspaper articles or seminars on the findings of the thesis research, as well as those who have joined groups of leavers we have coordinated. The combined information drawn from these conversations, discussions, letters and e-mails is used here to further validate the formal research findings. No count was made of the number of people who have contributed in this way, but it seems likely, on reflection, that it was well in excess of 500.

To the formal interview analysis and the more general collection of leavers' stories I have added my field notes and understandings from many participant observations of church services, church leadership meetings and conferences. Coupled with these are the field notes from a number of visits to groups of church leavers, such as the post-church group set up by Stuart and Michelle. However, while the substance of this argument will draw on the research base, it also draws heavily on my experience as a church attender and minister and the relationships formed in a group called Spirited Exchanges.[4]

This study draws together different strands of information, from formal research conditions and analysis through to information drawn from anecdotal conversations. All this information is then distilled through the eyes of someone who is both a church minister and sociologist. It is in this curious mix of sources and research perspectives that the depth of these findings is located.

At this point it is important to comment a little on my own involvement. I have been involved in evangelical, Pentecostal and charismatic churches for over 20 years, the last 12 of these as a minister within two such churches. So while the argument presented here is drawn from those who have left the church and is analysed through sociological research methods, there is also a deep commitment to and involvement with the very streams of the church that the subjects of this book have chosen to leave. Spirited Exchanges is a growing network of church leavers and those on the edges of the church who find the general church diet irrelevant, unhelpful or simply implausible from the perspective of their present experience. Many are people of deep Christian faith who are longing to continue and develop in their faith. The Spirited Exchanges group offers these faith journeyers an open forum to talk with others and in which to struggle together outside the normal structures we call church. It is a group that I greatly enjoy belonging to and one that continues to teach me much.

Previous research of church leavers has been based predominantly on large quantitative studies drawn from census or survey data. A recent extensive study of this type headed by Dr Peter Brierley found that 'whereas 12 % (5.4 million) of the English population went to church weekly each Sunday in 1979, and 10% (4.7 million) in 1989, this has dropped to 7.5% (3.7 million) in 1998' (Brierley, 2000, p. 13). If this rate were extrapolated out until 2016 it would indicate that less than 1 per cent of the British population would be at church. While Brierley sees this as a worst-case scenario and one that he believes is unlikely to eventuate, he nevertheless says that the study

> shows a haemorrhage akin to a burst artery. The country is littered with people who used to go to church but no longer do. We could well bleed to death. The tide is running out. At the present rate of change we [British churches] are one generation from extinction. (Brierley, 2000, p. 236)

Figures like these have lead to an increased interest in church leavers and church decline. Richter and Francis (1998, p. vii) suggest that why people are currently leaving the churches is the foremost question confronting the churches today. This is a huge shift from when Brinkerhoff and Burke (1980), and Bromley and associates (1988, p. 81) indicated that there was little research focusing on those who leave church. Slowly we are realizing the importance of research into why people are leaving the church and where they go.

Over recent years three popular texts have focused on studies of church leavers. In 1993 two books were published. William Hendricks' *Exit Interviews: Revealing Stories of Why People are Leaving the Church* reported in 1993 on the accounts of a 'couple of dozen' people interviewed in the United States who had left various churches. Michael Fanstone's *The Sheep that Got Away: Why People Leave the Church* (also in 1993) analysed 509 people randomly surveyed in shopping malls and other public places across England who had left a Christian church. Then in 1998 Richter and Francis published *Gone but Not Forgotten: Church Leaving and Returning*. In this study Richter and Francis used a combination of 27 in-depth face-to-face interviews and over 400 questionnaires drawn from a scientifically selected sample group. The information generated from the interviews and questionnaires was then used to test eight different theories on why people leave churches. Each of these studies has raised awareness of the importance of church leavers and provided readers with an increased understanding in an area where previously few guiding lights had been available.

The present study seeks to build on those mentioned above, yet it is also distinct in a number of ways:

1 This study is based on in-depth face-to-face interviews with more than 100 leavers and 50 church leaders. This means the research has a strong qualitative base.

2 The research participants in this study were all strongly committed adult members of evangelical, Pentecostal or charismatic churches.

3 This study focused both on why people left and more significantly how their faith changed and developed after leaving.

4 This research suggests a way of understanding both why many of the leavers have left their churches and what could have helped them to stay.

5 This research suggests ways individual leavers and groups of leavers can be encouraged to continue to develop their Christian faith and how the groups of leavers can helpfully engage in dialogue with churches as they find themselves increasingly in a new cultural context – the context of the so-called postmodern world.

David Tomlinson's best seller – *The Post-Evangelical* – also needs to be mentioned. While the previous texts have been based on research data, *The Post-Evangelical* is based on Tomlinson's own vast experience in evangelical churches and para-church groups. Tomlinson points to a growing dissatisfaction with evangelicalism among many immersed in our increasingly postmodern culture. Tomlinson's insight and analysis have greatly helped our understanding of the issues behind many people's decision to leave and provided an understanding of the increasing mismatch between popular forms of church and a postmodern social context.

Any study of church leavers[5] must begin by locating ex-church attenders. Tracking those who leave is not an easy task as church leavers quickly become part of a hidden group in society. Because of this, locating potential interviewees was initially quite problematic. However, once word of my interest in this area had slowly filtered out, there was no shortage of people to interview. Within the first year of the thesis research I had the names, addresses and contact phone numbers of far more potential interviewees than I could ever have interviewed.

The bulk of the interviewing phase of the research was carried out over three years (1994–6) principally with New Zealanders, although there are also a number of interviews with people outside New Zealand. The interviews were in-depth, face-to-face and taped. From these tape recordings verbatim transcripts were produced. Each of the interview transcripts was then analysed in its totality as the account of individuals' stories, and also subdivided into hundreds of specific topic categories. These categories were analysed, compared and contrasted in the formation of a detailed understanding of the faith trajectories of those who leave the Christian church. On average the interviews lasted around one and a half to two hours and included questions covering how each person came to be involved in a Christian church, the ways they became committed and how this commitment to Christ and the church was lived out, as well as questions looking at how and why they came to leave and their subsequent faith journey outside of their church.

Using a face-to-face interviewing method allows for questioning in much greater detail than is possible in a written or telephone survey. Because these interviews were primarily conducted in the interviewees' homes in a relaxed conversational manner I was able to pick up on the hesitations, gestures and underlying feelings of the interviewees and explore these for a richer understanding of experience and faith journey. It is important to state that all interviewees used here have been assigned pseudonyms and where necessary other potentially identifying information (e.g. locations) has been changed to ensure the confidentiality of those who voluntarily contributed their stories. It is because of their honesty, openness and willingness to allow the intimate details of their lives and faith to be probed, taped, analysed and dissected that their stories can be told. The assigned pseudonyms have been allocated only once so readers can trace the comments of each interviewee throughout the book.

Evangelical, Pentecostal and charismatic (EPC) church leavers

The evangelical, Pentecostal and charismatic stream of the Christian church, simplified here to the initials EPC, is growing phenomenally across the world. As Wagner has rightly stated, 'In all human history, no other non-political, non-militaristic, voluntary human movement has grown as rapidly as the Pentecostal/charismatic movement in the last 25 years' (in Synan, 1992, p. ii). Yet while EPC churches are growing rapidly it appears, at least in the West, that these same churches also have a wide-open back door through which the disgruntled, disillusioned and disaffiliated leave. In the wake of rising pluralism and growing societal scepticism towards the Christian faith such leave-taking appears to be increasing.

Despite the almost mantra-like status of the statement 'people are leaving the church', there appears to be little understanding of who leaves, when they leave, why they leave, and what happens to them and their faith after they leave. Of course, everyone has their own view on these issues but few – especially, it would seem, EPC church leaders – have taken the time to move beyond the stereotypes of the typical backsliding leaver in order to understand the real leavers' journeys. The argument that will be presented here is that the cause of leaving is rooted in the church, in society and in the individual leavers. In the interrelationship of the individual faith journeys, church theology and practice and the influence of the wider societal context can be found relations that make sense of why particular people leave particular churches at particular times. This interrelationship also provides a framework for understanding these leavers' post-church faith journeys.

However, before we move to consider the influence of these factors we need to come face to face with those who leave and realize something of their commitment to their Christian faith and the church. In many respects Stuart and Michelle were typical of the leavers I met over the three years of interviewing and have continued to meet since completing that research.

The people I interviewed had all made adult (over the age of 18) commitments to their Christian faith and to their respective EPC churches.

Ninety-eight had left the church for at least six months and were at the time of the interview not attending or involved in any church. Ten more interviews were made with those who were on the margins of their church. This group had not made a final decision to leave but they were very much on the edge and contemplating their exit.

The leavers interviewed were predominantly in their middle adult years (thirties and forties – see Table 1.1), in full-time employment (73 per cent), married (79 per cent) and with dependent children (80 per cent).

Table 1.1 Age range of interviewees

Age	Female		Male		Total	
	No.	%	No.	%	No.	%
20–25	–	–	1	2	1	1
25–30	2	3	1	2	3	3
30–35	8	14	7	14	15	14
35–40	23	40	14	28	37	34
40–45	18	31	21	42	39	35
45–50	2	3	2	4	4	4
50–55	3	5	2	4	5	5
55–60	1	2	2	4	3	3
60–65	1	2	–	–	1	1
Total	**58**		**50**		**108**	

While indications from previous research suggest that having children is a strong positive influence on church involvement,[6] the majority of leavers located through this research had dependent children. These leavers were choosing to cease their participation in a church despite the fact that this meant taking the children away from the socializing influence of the church and the provision of a nurturing environment for their children's Christian faith. Although some interviewees had continued to encourage their children to attend Sunday school or youth group, the children's attendance was generally short lived.

Twenty-eight per cent of the interviewees had, like Michelle, come from a strong church background. These people grew up attending church or church-based children's and youth groups and were supported in doing so by their parents. This parental support was evidenced by the parents' own regular church attendance. Forty per cent, like Stuart, came from nominal church backgrounds[7] where they as children had had some exposure to the church, although it was not a major influence on their parents' and families' lives. The remaining 30 per cent[8] came from non-churched backgrounds. These included people who grew up within other faiths, agnostic or atheistic family backgrounds, or families that held some belief but no affiliation to or attendance at church. As we saw in Michelle's case, 'Train a child in the way he should go, and when he is old he will not depart from it' (Proverbs 22.6) may be true of people's belief systems but it bears little correlation with continued church involvement.

Involvement in their EPC churches

The interviewees had on average been involved as adults in their respective EPC churches for over 15 years. A number were involved in churches, Sunday schools or church-based youth groups prior to their eighteenth birthday but these involvements were not recorded as part of their adult involvement.[9] The vast majority of interviewees had also held at least one, if not a number of key leadership positions within their church. Table 1.2 gives a breakdown of these positions. Beyond this church involvement many took part in leadership roles within para-church organizations. Only six of those interviewed were not involved in any of the leadership positions identified in Table 1.2.[10] This means 94

Table 1.2 Leadership positions held by interviewees

Involvements	Male		Female		Total	
	No.	%	No.	%	No.	%
Leadership of church	34	68	24	41	58	54
Leading home group	34	68	42	72	76	70
Leading youth work	27	54	24	41	51	47
Leading children's work	6	12	21	36	27	25
Leading worship	20	40	15	26	35	32
Leading prayer groups	29	58	29	50	58	54
Leading evangelistic programmes	28	56	24	41	52	48

per cent of the interviewees held at least one significant leadership position within their church.

The degree of the interviewees' commitment is further emphasized by considering the number who were involved in either full-time work within an EPC church or para-church group[11] or studied theology full-time.[12] In fact, 40 per cent of those interviewed were involved either in full-time study or full-time Christian work[13] (see Table 1.3). Added to this were a number who had undertaken full-time Christian study for less than a year, typically three to six months (ten people). There is also a further group involved in part-time theological study (seven people). Taken together, 33 per cent (36 people) of those interviewed had at some point undertaken full-time or part-time theological study.

Table 1.3 Those involved in full-time Christian work and/or full-time theological study

	Male		Female		Total	
	No.	%	No.	%	No.	%
Full-time Christian work	15	32	20	33	35	32
Full-time theological study	11	20	10	17	20	19

Even when those who had been involved in full-time capacities (work and/or study) are removed from the table of involvement in church leadership positions, the degree of participation in key roles remains very

Table 1.4 Voluntary involvement in key leadership positions[14]

Involvements	Male		Female		Total	
	No.	%	No.	%	No.	%
Leadership of church	20	60	9	28	29	45
Leading home groups	18	55	22	69	40	61
Leading youth work	16	48	11	34	27	42
Leading children's work	4	12	8	25	12	18
Leading worship	10	30	10	31	20	31
Leading prayer groups	14	42	10	31	24	37
Leading evangelistic programmes	13	40	7	22	20	31
Total	**33**		**32**		**65**	

high. Sixty per cent (65 people) of those interviewed had *not* been involved in full-time study or work roles. A breakdown of the leadership roles of those not involved in paid Christian work or full-time study is given in Table 1.4.

The average time the leavers had been out of church participation when I came to interview them was three and a half years.

Having introduced the leavers there are four comments that can be made, which challenge many of the commonly held stereotypes of the backsliding church leaver:

1 The interviewees were *not* leaving 'mainline' or 'traditional' churches but were leaving EPC churches. These churches are among the growing streams of the Christian church worldwide.
2 The interviewees were *not* leaving in the process of entering adulthood or even early adulthood but were predominantly leaving between 30 and 45 years of age.
3 The interviewees were *not* on the fringe of the church, but formed its very core. The vast majority held key leadership positions (94 per cent), and a large percentage (40 per cent) were involved in either full-time Christian study or work – many were involved in both.
4 The interviewees were *not* involved in the church for short periods of time. In fact the sample of interviewees involved in this research had been adult participants in EPC churches for an average of 15.8 years.

There is another, perhaps the most important, point that we also need to keep in mind. That is the majority of these leavers are not moving to a position of apostasy (i.e. no longer holding to the Christian faith), but like Stuart and Michelle are retaining their faith while leaving the church. They are also unlikely to return to an EPC church.

Leaving the Christian church but not the Christian faith

The majority of the people I met while doing this research and since completing it do not easily fit the common understandings about church leavers. They were not the stereotypical church leavers I expected to meet when I began the study. Nor are they easily fitted into a secularization argument drawn from prevalent understandings within the sociology of religion. Rather, their uniqueness is in the way they have moved outside the church but, as seen in the case of Stuart and Michelle, nevertheless claim to have continued in their Christian faith.

The argument presented, as already indicated, will concentrate on three distinct but interrelated factors which in combination provide an understanding of leavers from EPC churches. The three factors we need to consider are:

1 The changing societal culture that contemporary Western dwellers find themselves in; specifically this time of transition between the erosion of influence of modernity and the increasing influence of postmodernity.
2 The structure, beliefs and faith practices of EPC churches.
3 The faith development of individuals located within EPC churches and significantly influenced by societal changes brought with the transition to an increasingly postmodernist society.

It is in the dynamic interrelationship of these three factors that we can make sense of why people leave EPC churches and what happens to their faith after leaving.

This first chapter has provided an introduction to the EPC church leavers whose journeys will be woven into the following chapters. Stuart and Michelle are typical of the leavers we will meet. They left the EPC church to which they had been highly committed for over ten years without quarrel or incident, and moved to a non-church-based faith. Their reasons for doing this involved a number of factors – personal, church structural, faith and wider societal influences. When Michelle and Stuart left the church they became part of a group of similarly dissatisfied people who met fortnightly to talk, have breakfast together and sometimes pray or consider the Bible together. Michelle and Stuart are also typical of the wider group of leavers as they are both well educated[15] and creative people who were leaders in their church. They have a family which they are concerned for and for whom they want a positive Christian influence, and yet they remain outside of any church involvement. Michelle and Stuart present a human face to the back-door losses of the EPC churches.

A book in two halves

This book is in two halves because it seeks to cover two agendas. First, to give a framework of understanding for church leavers and people interested in those who leave the church. This framework involves meeting the leavers (Chapter 1), becoming aware of the characteristics of the churches they leave (Chapter 2), understanding the process through which they leave (Chapter 3) and being aware of the various faith trajectories of those who leave (Chapters 4–7). It is hoped that these chapters will provide a credible framework of understanding in an area where there is much misunderstanding, loose stereotypes, often downright ignorance and sometimes arrogant misjudgements.

The second section of the book (Chapters 8–11) focuses on providing resources for leavers and groups of people interested in church leavers. In Chapter 8 a map is given, which indicates a progression in people's faith journeys outside the church. Chapter 9 offers resources to leavers while Chapter 10 looks at what churches could do to stem the flow of leavers and support the faith of those who have already left. In the final chapter, Chapter 11, a possible discussion between EPC churches and leavers is given as a direction for the future.

NOTES

1 Para-church groups are umbrella mission organizations, which include people from many denominational backgrounds. Examples of such groups include Youth With a Mission (YWAM), Youth for Christ (YFC) or the Navigators.

2 A fictional pseudonym for the church they started. The real names of people and churches have been changed in order to maintain the confidentiality of those interviewed.

3 As part of the research I was able to interview one of these couples and the husband from the second couple independently.

4 Spirited Exchanges is a group that provides a forum for discussion and dialogue around issues that typically concern church leavers. At the time of writing it had been running for two and a half years on a weekly basis.

5 The Gallup Organization define the 'unchurched' American as 'someone who has not attended services in the previous six months other than for special religious holidays, weddings, funerals or the like'. Richter and

Francis, in *Gone but Not Forgotten* (1998, p. 10), adopted D. Hoge's definition of the church drop-out as someone who has reduced their church attendance to less than six times a year (not including Christmas, Easter, weddings or funerals). In this study, leavers had all been outside the church for six months or more with an average time outside the church of 3.5 years.

6 Roof states that 'unquestionably, the most frequently cited reasons [for people returning to church] have to do with family life. The influence of a spouse and keeping harmony within the family are strong factors, but far more important is the religious upbringing of children. The presence of young, school-age children and feelings of parental responsibility for them drives boomers back to church and to enrol their children in religious education classes' (1993, pp.156–7). Hoge *et al.* (1993, p. 246) agree, saying that of those who drop out from church and later return the highest reason (27 per cent) was related to concern for their children and family life.

7 The word 'nominal' is used in a broad sense to mean those children raised in families that encouraged or supported their children's participation in church activities, but where the parents were not involved themselves in more than a nominal sense, i.e. attended less than monthly.

8 These percentages have been rounded.

9 The active adult involvement of the people I interviewed ranged from three to 30 years.

10 Four were married to spouses who did hold significant leadership positions in the church and saw themselves as supporting their spouse in this position.

11 Those involved for 12 months or more as overseas missionaries are also included in this grouping.

12 To satisfy this criterion, the person needed to be either working or studying full-time for at least one year.

13 As some were involved in both full-time study and full-time Christian work the total is less than indicated in Table 1.3.

14 This table relates to interviewees who were *not* involved in full-time Christian work or study. The totals in bold print indicate the number of men and women in key leadership roles. Many were involved in more than one role.

15 Michelle has a tertiary diploma and Stuart is a medical doctor.

TWO

EPC churches

In the previous chapter we met Stuart and Michelle who are in many respects typical of leavers from EPC churches. These are people who have made adult commitments to their Christian faith and to their respective churches, have been significantly involved in key leadership roles – many as full-time workers – and as Bible and theological students. On average these leavers have been active participants in their churches for over 15 years and yet they have left the church. In order to understand their decision to leave we need to also understand something of the character of the churches they leave. In this chapter we look at the types of churches they are leaving. The story of Gabrielle and Craig gives glimpses of the EPC style of church and the reasons people come to leave.

In the early 1970s Gabrielle moved from the small mainstream traditional church her family attended to go to a large Pentecostal church which was then at the forefront of Pentecostal church growth in her city. The attraction of this new church was, in her words, the 'liberty and freedom' that it offered; there was more 'life' and 'vitality'. Gabrielle stayed there a few months and then moved to join a separate house church that was just beginning. She said of the house church, 'It seemed to be pertinent to young people and relevant. It seemed very loose at the time, certainly there was no structure.' This house group had about 50 people at its core and 400 to 500 around the fringes.

It was in this group that she met her husband Craig who with many others had joined the house group after being 'caught up in the whole Jesus movement of the 1970s'. Prior to this Craig had no church background, except a brief period in a Sunday school as a child, and had left home as a teenager to go surfing.

> *Craig* I had rejected all my parents' values and left home at a very early age. I just went surfing. So I just dropped out for a few years and then got caught up in the whole Jesus movement of the 1970s, when it first hit. Through

that I became a Christian in a very real way. I mean, it totally transformed my life. I'm still quite happy to acknowledge that to anybody. I have no qualms about that at all.

Initially the gatherings of the house group were pretty relaxed. Their meetings 'started out with singing, there would be long sessions of singing and informal praying . . . and witnessing – telling their stories'. At this stage the group was loosely advised by a couple of older men who gained the respect of the younger participants and could identify with the group. Craig remembers a key incident that typified one of these men.

> *Craig* The way he got the ear of the people in the group was illustrated by the story where he met a couple of the kids in town and recognized them as some of the ones who had drifted into the church occasionally just to look at what was going on, and had heard that they had been newly converted. He said, 'Hey, neat to see you again.' These guys were wandering through town with their long hair and hippie gear on and in bare feet and Mr Brown said, 'How sensible, why do I get around in shoes like this?' And in the middle of town took his shoes and socks off and said, 'This feels great.' He was a humble person, very gentle, but a listening person.

But not long after this the leadership of a larger Pentecostal church, who had been keeping a watchful eye on the development of the house group, suggested that they needed more of a structure.

> *Craig* That was when we started getting into the whole structure of the church thing. The experts saw that now was the time to step in and organize these people properly. They basically started forming us into a church structure with formalized leadership and that sort of thing. Initially it was voluntary people in leadership positions and senior people from the church in town that came out on a volunteer basis.

The move towards structure in the group mirrored a move for more structure and conformity within the lives of many of those who had joined the Jesus movement out of what he describes as the alternative culture of the period. Craig says of his friends:

> *Craig* The thing that I used to notice was dress code. You know, here's a bunch of hippies from the sixties. We were really in the fringe element, into the drug scene and really weird and wacky, those sort of guys, and the next minute they were in suits and ties. These were my friends.

The changes brought about by Craig's conversion were not as severe for him as they had been for his friends, at least as far as he saw it. Craig carried on surfing and didn't make any outward changes to his appearance. He did, however, move back to his parents' home and begin training towards a future job. This was a result of a desire to marry Gabrielle, who wanted him to get an education. Although Craig came out of the alternative culture Gabrielle had never been a part of that scene. Craig and Gabrielle reflected the membership of the house group – many from the alternative cultural scene of the time and others who had moved from traditional church backgrounds into the perceived life, freedom and vitality of the Pentecostal churches.

The next move for the house group was a further step along the road to formal church structures. This occurred when the leaders of the house group decided they needed a pastor, though initially this was to be on a part-time basis. The man they got was a young pastor who had worked in a growing Pentecostal church. Gabrielle describes him, saying:

> *Gabrielle* . . . a very goal-oriented person. He had a go-ahead business background. He had a real zeal for wanting to establish a big church, having been part of a church that had really grown in leaps and bounds. So he very much wanted the same thing for the church here . . . he was a very charismatic leader . . . so it grew and became one of the happening churches with lots of people coming along.

Gabrielle and Craig remained significantly involved in this church for 10 years before moving on to another church in the early 1980s when this pastor and his direction for the church began to part company with what they saw as being important. Up until then they were house group leaders, part of the church leadership, and Gabrielle was very involved in counselling, praying for people and advising the pastor on people and church concerns.

In order to understand the church environment that Gabrielle and Craig had joined and would subsequently leave, we need to understand something of the influences that have formed the EPC stream of churches.

Characteristics of EPC churches

EPC churches can be considered as a single stream despite their individual distinctiveness and their various shapes and sizes. EPC churches overwhelmingly hold to a conservative form of evangelical theology; many, perhaps most, have been influenced in their worship and governance styles by the Pentecostal and charismatic movements and in their focus by the church growth movement. In order to understand the EPC churches we need to consider the impact of each of these movements in shaping this stream of church life. We also need to remember that this is one of the few growing church streams of the church today.

The influence of the evangelical movement on EPC church life

Evangelicalism is today the dominant and growing face of Christianity across the globe. The old divisions between liberalism and fundamentalism have given way, fundamentalism having been subsumed as one subset of the larger conservative evangelical stream and liberalism having suffered a gradual numerical demise. Alister McGrath, an evangelical Anglican and Oxford theology professor, writes of the evangelical movement:

> Evangelicalism, once regarded as marginal, has now become mainline. It can no more be dismissed as an insignificant sideshow, sectarian tendency, or irrelevance to the life of the churches. It has moved from the wings to centre stage, displacing others once regarded as mainline, and who consequently feel deeply threatened and alienated by this development. Its commitment to evangelism has resulted in numerical growth, where some other variants of Christianity are suffering from severe contraction. (McGrath, 1994, p.9)

Today the term 'evangelical' has become a very popular self-designation. For example, none of the senior pastors I spoke with described either themselves or their church as 'fundamentalist', each preferring to call themselves 'evangelical'. 'Evangelicalism' has also become an umbrella term for a vast host of theological and culturally distinct groups. As a 1982 *Newsweek* article (26 April) says, 'So many different kinds of

Christians now call themselves evangelical that the label has lost any precise meaning.' Although a precise definition cannot be given, David Bebbington, perhaps the leading writer in the area, states that

> There are four qualities that have been the special marks of Evangelical religion: *conversionism*, the belief that lives need to be changed; *activism*, the expression of the gospel in effort; *biblicism,* a particular regard for the Bible; and what may be called *crucicentrism,* a stress on the sacrifice of Christ on the cross. Together they form a quadrilateral of priorities that is the basis of Evangelicalism. (Bebbington, 1989, pp. 2–3)

In a similar way McGrath sees evangelicalism as being 'based on a cluster of six controlling convictions, each of which is regarded as being true, of vital importance, and grounded in scripture.' These six fundamental convictions are:

1 The supreme authority of scripture as a source of knowledge of God, and a guide to Christian living.
2 The majesty of Jesus Christ, both as incarnate God and Lord, and as the saviour of sinful humanity.
3 The lordship of the Holy Spirit.
4 The need for personal conversion.
5 The priority of evangelism for both individual Christians and the church as a whole.
6 The importance of the Christian community for spiritual nourishment, fellowship and growth. (McGrath, 1994, p. 51)

Although evangelicalism comes in many forms and is best seen as an umbrella term under which a variety of subtypes are linked, the predominant form prevalent in EPC churches is a conservative evangelicalism that has close theological links with fundamentalism. That is, these churches lie close to the theological understandings of Christian fundamentalism. The EPC churches' teaching reflects more literalistic readings of Scripture, which allow little space for the insights of critical approaches to exegesis, although many within EPC churches would want to distance themselves from the 'biblical inerrancy' of fundamentalism. There is, nevertheless, a clear dependence on an uncritical reading of the Bible as an external authority in matters of belief and ethics. From their evangelical heritage, EPC churches have a strong focus on evangelism, seeing people come out of the 'world' and into the 'church'. Such a focus on conversionism is based on the individual's decision. This emphasis has reduced the priority for the issues of social justice, political concerns and the ongoing development of an individual's faith beyond the point of conversion and the process of early discipleship.

It is debatable how much conservative evangelicalism differs from fundamentalism. Brian Gilling, a New Zealand researcher, states:

> Many Christians, calling themselves evangelicals, hold theological positions identical to fundamentalism's, but would shudder at the thought of being tarred with the fundamentalist brush. Their problem may be with the attitude adopted by fundamentalists of strict separatism from all potentially tainting influences. Or it may have to do with difficulty in assenting to strict biblical inerrancy, although the Bible is still held in high regard as possessing ultimate authority in all matters of faith and practice. The line between fundamentalism and such 'conservative evangelicalism' is a fine one. (Gilling, 1992, p. xi)

The Pentecostal and charismatic movements

In many countries the evangelical, Pentecostal and charismatic movements have been closely linked. The rise of the evangelical movement led to much of the expansion of the Pentecostal churches in the 1960s, while Pentecostalism, which began at the beginning of the twentieth century, laid a foundation for the charismatic movement of the late 1960s and early 1970s. The net result is that 'the evangelical movement has been highly charismaticized', as David Tomlinson states.

David Barrett defines Pentecostals as 'Christians who are members of explicitly Pentecostal denominations whose major characteristic is a rediscovery of, and new experience of, the supernatural with a powerful and energising ministry of the Holy Spirit' (Barrett, 1988, p. 124). Charismatics too describe themselves as having been renewed in the Spirit but can be distinguished from Pentecostals because they 'remain within their older mainline non-Pentecostal denominations' (Barrett, 1998, pp. 125–6). Theologically and experientially the Pentecostal and charismatic movements are very similar, their main point of difference being whether they form independent churches or remain within traditional church structures. Because of the similarities of the two and their link with evangelical theology I have combined them as a common stream of the Christian church – the EPC churches.

One of the great attractions of the EPC churches is the extended family feel that they exude. There is a sense of warmth, family and community offered to new people. This big, caring and loving family environment has proved to be very attractive to many young adults and older hurt adults.

The Pentecostal and charismatic movements brought a new culture of worship based on contemporary music styles, electric instruments, overhead projection of words, free praise and open prayer times. While these are the most obvious and dramatic changes they are less significant than the radical changes to church service structure away from a liturgically based service that incorporated confession, intercession, meditation, silence, hymns and prayers rich in the history and tradition of the Christian church, to the individual-focused, freewheeling worship of the Pentecostal and charismatic movements. This involved a subtle but definite shift in worship from the focus on the church of history and the God of eternity to a focus on the needs, wants and concerns of the individual church attender. In many respects such changes reflected the mood of society in its increasing individualism.

If the charismatic and Pentecostal movements were to change the forms and focus of worship they were equally to affect the patterns of leadership and decision-making within churches. The previous emphasis on theological training and ministerial induction began to give way to charismatic leadership based on exceptional qualities or personal giftings. The new church leaders were those who were strong teachers, prophets and leaders. Ironically the power given to these leaders was arguably much greater than that of the minister or priest in a traditional mainstream church. The charismatic and Pentecostal movements brought in their wake an authoritarian leadership style that expected leaders to lead and tended to give their congregations little say in decision-making.

The new EPC churches were successful in drawing young people caught up in the Jesus movement and counterculture movements of the 1960s and early 1970s and also attracting church attenders from traditional structures, who were looking for a clearer, more biblically based theology and freer worship and church structures.

EPC churches and EPC church people found that they had much in common and could easily identify with each other. After all, they held in common a conservative evangelical theology and a similar experience of the work of the Holy Spirit. There was also the uniting influence of a number of para-church groups, which bridged people from across EPC churches. These groups served to link Christians from evangelical, Pentecostal and charismatic churches as well as other streams of the church. For example, the influence of para-church groups such as Youth With A Mission and Youth For Christ helped link Christians from across the spectrum of EPC churches.

The church growth movement

The 'church growth' movement's origin stems from the heart of evangelicalism itself – a concern to evangelize the peoples of the world effectively. Donald McGavran, the initiator of the movement and a third-generation missionary, was concerned that most missionary church endeavours were only growing at around 11 per cent per decade. However, some he observed were growing much faster than this, at a rate of 100 to 200 per cent each decade. McGavran began asking what the fast-growing missions did that the others weren't doing. The lessons he learned from his study of mission growth were later to form the underlying principles of his teaching on church growth. The principal focus of the movement was the local church, because McGavran believed that God's kingdom on earth would grow through the growth of the local church. McGavran and the church growth literature argued that church effectiveness in growth could be assessed using the research tools of the social sciences. The language and tools of the social sciences ('growth goals' and the methods of management, marketing and quantitative social research techniques) brought openness to the process of assessing church growth and became part of the language and focus of church pastors. New books and seminars abounded, identifying vital signs of churches that grow and practical methods to increase the number of people choosing to be part of your church.

The latest phase of the church growth movement has been the rising prominence of mega-churches (churches with well over 1,000 people attending). The leaders of these churches have often been seen as guides and gurus for church leaders and pastors. Perhaps the leading example presently is the Willow Creek Community Church in Chicago, which is now the largest church in the United States. The influence of this church and its methods has been enhanced by the development of Willow Creek Associations in other countries, which provide tapes, videos and books and arrange seminars from the teaching staff at Willow Creek Church for interested church leaders.

The focus of the church growth movement – adding more people – has led to churches concentrating on programmes, service styles and facilities that meet the demands of potential new believers and attenders. Seeker-sensitive services, one of the catchphrases of the Willow Creek Church, exemplifies this concern. These services are developed with 'unchurched' people in mind. Such services are structured to make those who are new to church feel comfortable and help them to connect with the theme of the service. Often churches put enormous amounts of time, leadership energy and money into making their church more seeker-sensitive. In this way they are enlarging the front door of the church, through which they hope new people will come to Christian faith and become members of their church.

In summary, EPC churches are churches that have been shaped by the combined influence of conservative evangelical theology, the worship and church governance styles of the charismatic and Pentecostal movements, and that have taken on the techniques of growth espoused in the church growth movement. Such churches' characters, structures, programmes and focuses are the derivatives of these movements. To fully understand the stories of the leavers of EPC churches it is important to understand the common features of the churches they leave. Of course, each local church has its own ethos and character, which has been influenced to differing degrees by each of the movements discussed above as well as its own local context.

While we are focusing attention on the church it is important to comment on the title of this book – *A Churchless Faith*. This title is intended as both an engaging catchphrase and as something of a misnomer. It is a catchphrase that connects with the lived experience of many people who see themselves as people of Christian faith but who are also completely alienated from the institutionalized church. A reader of the Australasian edition has commented on reading the book in a local café at a large shopping mall. As he read he was interrupted by a shop owner who saw the title and said, 'That's me'. The man had not had anything to do with the book; he simply saw the title as an apt description of his own experience. In this sense it is a title that points to something that increasingly resonates with many people. We must also remember that a churchless faith is theologically a misnomer. All followers of Christ (Christians, from the Greek *christianoi* = 'Christ people') are by definition part of the 'church' – the house or community of the Lord (from the Greek *Kyriake* = belonging to *Kyrios*, Lord). That is the church universal, the church made up of all those who belong to Christ. Such people may or may not presently be actively involved in a local community of 'Christ's people' – the local church. But the title also pushes us further as we will, in later chapters, consider the groups formed by church leavers that are offering new ways of being the local church.

THREE

The leaving process

Jane had been deeply committed to a number of Pentecostal churches prior to leaving the church in which her husband was an assistant pastor. She originally became involved in Pentecostal churches through a friend who had taken her along to one as a teenager. Initially Jane was fully supportive of the church and the EPC faith that it represented. Yet after a number of years as an assistant pastor's wife and missionary (with her husband) she began to distance herself from the church. It was a process of leaving which, for Jane, took over ten years.

> *Jane* I would have got involved in church about 1973 and stayed with this particular church heavily until 1990. But the last ten years I was disengaging and I would have been out a lot earlier if it hadn't been for my marriage. I just basically hung in there for that . . . and it was quite a long time.

Throughout this time the church leaders were trying to help Jane to cease her questioning and her sense of not fitting and to be an active part of the church community. Jane mentioned on two or three occasions throughout the interview that she was trying to fit in, trying to comply: 'I did try, I really did try, but I couldn't go against what I felt was wrong in certain situations.' At times the church leadership was helpful to her. At other times the hierarchy would call her in to meetings to be spoken to. As she said, 'I was constantly on the mat. Constantly being hauled up.'

When I asked her what the purpose of these leadership meetings was when they 'put her on the mat' she replied:

> *Jane* The purpose, I think was to try and get me to comply and come over to their way of thinking, and be one of them. It was a sense of that they all thought a certain way and I didn't and I needed to adjust and be like them.

Despite her own efforts to try to fit in and the pressure of the church leadership to help her or at times seemingly force her to comply, Jane continued to feel out of place in the church. At one point Jane was 'taken under the wing of the pastor's wife' but that too failed to alleviate the rumbling sense of dissatisfaction within. In some cases Jane's questioning was quite explicit and in others it was a determination not to be told how to behave.

> *Jane* My kids went through a stage of wanting to wear jeans. The church preferred children to wear trousers to church, and I was told at the time that my children were not to wear jeans to church because it was a bad example. I basically refused, because I had always gone by my own instincts as far as being a parent was concerned. I never bought into their thing about parents being the boss, and all that. I had been to a few parenting seminars where they were really into discipline and everything. I used to get really angry and churned up about that kind of thing. So it was a constant battle.

Realizing that she was beginning to move out of the church Jane started a university course and built support networks for herself outside the church. Then for over a year she stopped attending the church services. This created difficulties for the family and for her husband in particular. Jane then tried to make herself attend, if only for the children. Eventually the pastor became concerned about her non-attendance as it was being picked up by a number of people in the church. He came around to see her at her home and tried to make a compromise with her. In the agreement he would accept that she wasn't cut out to be a pastor's wife and release her from those obligations, if she would come to the Sunday services.

But by now Jane knew that church was becoming 'very destructive' for her. 'Over the last few years I was just really stuck, and I knew that I was stuck, and I wasn't going anywhere. And I think too I was hungry for knowledge and I wanted to move on.' However, Jane was aware that this wasn't the same for everyone in the church:

> *Jane* A lot of people don't experience that and are just happy to be in that structure that is functioning well, and that could be OK. But it didn't work for me, because I questioned too many things, and I couldn't accept the theology.

Eventually in her desperation Jane reached a point of decision.

> *Jane* I remember one day thinking I'm going to get out of this, I'm not going to be stuck here the rest of my life. I don't care what it takes, I don't care if I lose my marriage, and I remember saying to God I don't care if I lose you,

or whatever the cost is I'm going to do it. It was something I decided in spite of myself. It was sort of a turning point for me really.

But in the end she did go back to church, if only to be with the family for the Christmas service. Once there she had to listen to the message, on this occasion a joint message given by two people who she remembers 'berating' the congregation.

> *Jane* It should have been a nice joyous service, but the pair of them went on and on. They just talked too much drivel, talked absolute nonsense. I went home and basically picked the sermon to bits, and I said to my husband I'm not ever going back to that church. I've left. That's it. I never went back and I never thought, 'Oh, I've done the wrong thing.'

Although Jane never went back to that church she did attend a small, theologically liberal church for two years.

> *Jane* It was just completely different, it was high church, it was completely non-threatening. They were quite liberal and eclectic. I mean, I couldn't have coped with anything that had pressed any buttons. It was more that I needed some sort of church family because I'd lost 99 per cent of my support network. So I really had this as a kind of bridge, a transitional stage when I went to this little church. But I wasn't that involved, not in the same way.

When I interviewed Jane she no longer attended services at this or any other church. Rather she sees her energy going into her studies, family and the voluntary health association of which she is a part. Jane's story exemplifies the process of leaving undertaken by the interviewees. Her story does, however, have one exceptional feature – the length of time she took to leave. For the majority of interviewees the leaving process was condensed in time to approximately a two-year period. Jane's exit took longer because there were many factors that held her in the church. These included her husband's job as a pastor, her young children and her marriage. Although Jane's story in this regard is exceptional, it does highlight the journey of leaving undertaken, albeit more quickly, by the majority of church leavers interviewed. It is a process that has various phases. Knowing and being able to recognize these phases can be helpful for the individual to give understanding of what could be happening to them and where it could be leading. It could also be helpful for church leaders who are observing people in the 'leaving process'.

31

The process of leaving

The vast majority of those who were interviewed did not leave their church suddenly. In fact, they indicated a gradual process of reflection, questioning and withdrawal which lasted many months or years prior to their decision to leave. They drifted out of the church, often realizing only in hindsight that they had left. Because of the nature of church participation it is possible to drift out on a trial basis, or change your attendance patterns to the point of being increasingly less regular at church events. It is the voluntary nature of church participation and the potential reversibility of the decision that makes such an imperceptible leave-taking possible. A number spoke of a process of feeling dissatisfied, questioning and reducing their participation over a long period of time followed by a reduced frequency of church attendance to the point that they woke up one morning deciding they wouldn't go to church again. This was usually after not attending for some considerable period of time. In this sense it is a gradual drift out to the point of a retrospective decision that they have in fact left.

Some people did, however, leave more suddenly. Of this group, ten people spoke of a process of withdrawal that was already in progress prior to a significant event that encouraged their sudden leaving. Another 12 left suddenly (without indications of a prior process of withdrawal) through circumstances that they felt called for a rapid decision. Three of the twelve left during a marriage break-up, two left because their church had closed down, two were invited to join a post-church group that they thought was a good idea at the time, and two left quickly due to traumatic family and health concerns that they felt were not being addressed within the church. The final three left because of major difficulties within the church. Of these three, one couple left as a result of what they perceived to be overly autocratic leadership. The final person left the church after his wife had also left. It appears that while this may have been a sudden decision for him it was not for his wife.

Helen Ebaugh, an American sociologist and ex-nun, has written about the process of leaving important commitments, particularly the process of nuns who leave their vocation. Through her research she developed a way of understanding leaving by seeing it as a process with a number of discernible phases. Ebaugh describes a four-stage leaving process:

1 First doubts;
2 Seeking and weighing alternatives;
3 Negotiating turning points;
4 Developing a new sense of identity.

Here I will illustrate Ebaugh's first three phases with the accounts of leavers I interviewed from EPC churches.

FIRST DOUBTS

The doubting stage Ebaugh describes as 'essentially one of reinterpreting and redefining a situation that was previously taken for granted. First doubts involve a reinterpretation of reality, a realization that things are not what they seemed to be' (Ebaugh, 1988, p.41). This doubting can be triggered by a range of circumstances of which Ebaugh discusses four: organizational changes, burnout, disappointment or changes in relationships and events. This fourth grouping of events that spark the first doubts includes events that occur within both the organization and the individual.

For many of the interviewees an event or series of events in their own lives prompted a process of re-evaluating their continued participation in the church. Such events included a period of personal sickness, loss of a job, a career or geographical move, or beginning a new course of study that provided a differing view on life than that espoused by the church. Jane, for example, spoke of a number of trigger points in her own process of leaving that were intimately connected with her own internal struggle with the church and its faith. These included church structural events such as being called into leadership meetings to be spoken to. But they also included events in her personal life such as her hunger for knowledge and eventual decision to begin tertiary study, and going back to work.

Disillusionment with leaders or the church structure can be seen as a catalyst that acts as a trigger to the doubting phase. The doubting phase described by the majority of interviewees (56 per cent) indicates a disgruntledness or disenchantment that is more deeply and personally rooted. It was a disenchantment with the whole package of church. This is a far wider disillusionment than one particular event or aspect of church life. The following comments help to illustrate this:

Stuart I increasingly came to see that people were where they were at and I was where I was at, and it wasn't necessary for them to follow the same path that I was following or ask the questions I was asking. But I was never going to be satisfied within that sort of framework. Not that I was really actually looking for satisfaction, but it just came to a point where it was pointless really to continue . . . and for the first time this opportunity to be part of a group outside church came up. In a number of ways I actually felt free on the inside to lay church aside, which I never had before.

Paul There are probably two or three main things, I would think. One of them was just the growing dissatisfaction over a few years of, 'Is this all there is?' You seemed to be going over the same ground. And I would say not growing as a person, though I may not have said it in those words then. Social needs, just kind of the things that used to excite you, now you are doing them because that is what you have to do. Just in the whole service and the way of worship. And just a growing sense, I guess, of something just doesn't fit. I'm a round peg in a square hole sort of thing. Doors were being opened up to us to go full-time [as pastors in the church] if we liked. We were just not interested. It was kind of unusual at that stage to turn down opportunities that others were striving to get. So I couldn't put it in so many words except to say that I probably felt, 'This is no longer where we are at'.

John As I talk about my journey, and I do so quite openly, people say to me things like, 'Well, that's interesting because . . .' and they start to talk about themselves. I mean I go along with how everything is here, but personally I'm disgruntled. It's a word I have come across twice in the last two weeks, from two different people. The person last night was essentially saying that their spirituality had dried up, and they wanted to get out of the church. They were saying they go through this rote every week. They come to church twice on Sundays, sing the songs and listen to the messages but their spirituality has dried up. They want to get out and get to something, not just another church, but something that brings their spirituality alive again. That really means something to them, with a deep conviction. It is not just a routine you go through, this is what you are supposed to do, to be a good Christian and hang on in there until heaven comes [laughs]. They recognize that after 12 years in the ministry I obviously had some seriousness about my Christianity, so I'm not talking out of nowhere.

Ebaugh points out that in this first doubting phase the 'process is usually gradual in that the individual first experiences overall dissatisfaction in a generalized way and only eventually is able to specify and articulate what he or she finds lacking in the situation' (Ebaugh, 1988, p. 41). This points to the fact that before a person begins consciously to realize they are beginning to move out, the leaving process may have already been operating at a subconscious level for quite some time.

During this doubting phase people frequently give out clues that they are dissatisfied. Clues which may be noticed by others. For some the worship style they had previously spoken so positively about is now criticized. Others who used to be up near the front are now regularly sitting towards the back of the church – more as observers than participants. Those who were there every week are now beginning to miss a few Sundays for no apparent reason. The preaching they would previously have taken notes from and wouldn't have missed now seems irrelevant and fails to connect with them as it did in the past. For others the home group, prayer group, youth group or children's group they were once very excited about leading no longer carries any interest for them.

Of course we all have days, weeks, even months like this, but when the dissatisfaction lingers, and even seems to grow in intensity, it can mark the beginning of a withdrawal. For some this may eventually lead to them leaving church, but for others it can be a more internalized leaving.

SEEKING ALTERNATIVES

The second stage in Ebaugh's theory involves seeking alternatives. Here the individual intentionally considers alternative courses of action to remaining as an active church member. At this stage some weighing of the outcomes of various options will be undertaken.

> The process of seeking and evaluating alternatives is an interesting and complex one. As long as individuals are content in given roles, they are aware of numerous alternatives in a vague and general way. They have family, friends, and acquaintances engaged in all kinds of alternative roles. Through the media and casual conversation, these alternatives are known and perhaps even vicariously experienced. However, under conditions of personal dissa-

tisfaction with an existing role, vague alternatives take on a new perspective and focus (Ebaugh, 1988, p. 92).

Jane describes this process for herself, saying:

> *Jane* I didn't have the luxury of just being able to pull out in the way that people who weren't on the payroll could. But I certainly disengaged mentally and I started to build support networks outside of the church tentatively. I would go to university courses and things like that . . . And then I went to work, so I started to kind of make steps out without doing anything too drastically.

When weighing alternatives leads a person to consider leaving in further detail, people will often shift 'reference groups' as Jane began to do. Another means of weighing the alternatives may involve a period of re-hearsing what life would be like outside of church. This rehearsal can take place in two basic ways. Either by imagining what it would be like to no longer be involved in church (playing out the scenarios in your head), or perhaps by spending Sunday morning at the beach, with friends, going shopping, or sleeping in. In this way the person is able to 'trial' what it would be like not going to church every week.

Once a person moves this far down the leaving process the final decision is usually close at hand. As Ebaugh states,

> It is almost as though once people 'see the lights of the city, you can't keep them down on the farm.' If the alternative role is indeed a good 'fit' and the individual feels comfortable with the anticipated role expectations, the new role takes on an attraction and compelling force which serves to draw the person away from a current role; the 'pull' of the new role becomes an added incentive to the 'pushes' or dissatisfactions of the old one . . . all that remains is a final decision to make the transition. (Ebaugh, 1988, p. 117)

Seventeen per cent of interviewees spoke of a sense of no longer fitting in at church. Another 25 per cent spoke of a parting of the ways where what was important to them, and was their growing edge, was simply foreign to the concerns and focus of their church community. This promoted a sense of alienation between the church's focus and journey and their own.

> *Anthea* Another big crack-up was when I reverted to my maiden name. I mean, if I had gone out and committed adultery and come back and said

how really sorry I was about this there would have been openness and forgiveness. Because I dared to think for myself and choose to use my maiden name, and I was not sorry . . . there was a three-hour meeting with the leadership over that.

Pam I think one of the things that disturbed me greatly was when we got back from Amsterdam. As I remember it we walked into the middle of the debate about the legality of homosexual relationships. I was deeply disturbed by what I felt was incredible bigotry and prejudice that was coming out of the church at that stage. I suppose having lived in Amsterdam where there is a strong homosexual population and an awareness of those issues, and also friends and just my own personal understanding, I just felt sickened, yeah, really sickened by the kind of rhetoric, anti-homosexual rhetoric, that was being bandied around at that point. That for me was a major factor of my disillusionment with the Pentecostal church. There was this claptrap about you love the sinner but don't love the sin. I just felt that was incredibly false and insincere. And just the energy that there seemed to be in fighting homosexuality that came from the church. It was such a major priority for so many people. I felt that if people feel that is so important, and other issues that Christians should be addressing aren't, then I guess I felt very alienated. I don't belong in this group. I don't share those same kind of priorities. I felt very out of touch with it.

Emily I found out a little bit about the Palestinian history, and realized that the politicians that are in the Israeli parliament today, those very same people were terrorists, because they were bullying and killing people and shooting people in the name of God to get their land back. And people from my home church just kind of think the Jewish church got back their land. But in order to get back the land, they shot people and they killed them, bombed them and took the land back. The Israeli Government is still to this day occupying Arab land. And this is all in the name of God. I thought, 'How can I support this? This isn't love. How can I support this?' I began to get cross with people who supported it. So I went up there [Palestine] and made contacts and it just didn't add up to me at all. And this is blind support. I mean, my sister's one of them in particular. I mean, hey, 'What the Israelis do is fine.'

Ebaugh isolates a common feeling among leavers that may occur at different points in the process of leaving for the each individual which she calls the 'vacuum'. She says:

There is one emotional experience that characterizes over three-quarters of all those interviewed. The point in the process at which it occurred varied . . . Regardless of when it occurred, the majority of the interviewees went through a period of feeling anxious, scared, at loose ends, that they didn't belong. The experience is best described as a vacuum in that the people felt 'in midair', 'ungrounded', 'neither here nor there', 'nowhere'. (Ebaugh, 1988, p. 143)

Many church leavers spoke of having a sense of disenchantment and major faith-, theology- or church-based questions but at the same time being unable to leave for other reasons. This group represented 38 per cent of the leavers. For some people, like Jane, they were held by their job, or their spouse's job, within a specifically Christian organization or by their family needs (e.g. concern for children's Christian faith). Others were tied to continued church participation out of a fear of becoming like others they have seen who left the church and did not return. Often this is tied to a perception that such people 'lose their faith' in the process of leaving the church. Some of the leavers (9 per cent) spoke of staying but under severe duress and through considerable personal discomfort.

Jane But I had to go to church. The last year that we were there, that my husband was on the payroll, I didn't go to church at all. I couldn't. Saturday night I would work myself up and say, 'I've got to go to church tomorrow, I've got to go to church tomorrow.' And then on Sunday morning I would be sick, really sick. And then I just decided I wasn't going. And my kids, it was really awkward because they would get accosted. They went with my husband and they would get accosted in the main foyer. 'Where's mum? Why isn't she here?' And it became very awkward for them. So they used to pressure me to come as well.

Ruth I remember saying to these friends of mine that it is exactly the same feeling, when I think about going to church, that is exactly the same feeling as when I'm in Manchester and I look up and there is a bus coming towards me. And everything inside me says, 'Don't step out!' I have that exact feeling when I get up Sunday morning and wonder whether I should go to church. Everything inside me says, 'No'. And when I told friends at church about this they said, 'Do you think that is of the devil?'

In an attempt to resolve the growing sense of not fitting in, 14 per cent of leavers spoke of making a sideways move in their process of leaving. For some this was a move to teaching the children's programme that effectively removed them from the Sunday service. Others talked of moving church or trying a few different churches.

THE TURNING POINT

The third phase in Ebaugh's leaving process is the 'turning point'. Here the person, as Jane described in the last section, makes a firm decision to exit. For the majority of leavers the decision to leave involves an abrupt turning point associated with a specific event. Ebaugh speaks of five main types of events:

Specific events
These events crystallize a person's ambivalence. One example that Ebaugh gives is of a nun who left the convent after a new rule to stop smoking in the convent was introduced. Interestingly the nun was not herself a smoker.

The last straw
This is an event in a series of similar events that simply tips the person over the edge. One of the interviewees in this study talked of her final night at church (the night she finally decided to leave). She was sitting in the church when she began to read the newsletter and saw who was down to preach that night. She said that she just burst into tears realizing that she couldn't take another of his sermons and left. This was the last time she went to the church.

Time-related factors
Time-related factors include, for example, turning a particular age. One of the interviewees in this study indicated that turning 30 and still being single was a crucial point in her decision to leave the church.

Excuses
Here a person waits for a reason or excuse before they finally decide to leave (for example, a disagreement with a key leader).

Either/or alternatives
Where a person reaches a point where they must choose between one of two alternatives.

Turning points serve to mobilize the internal resources needed within the individual to finally leave. They act as final markers and announce the decision to leave. Forty-one per cent of leavers indicated that there was a

Table 3.1 Turning points in the final decision of leavers

Turning point in decision to leave	Number of interviewees
Knocked back by church	20
Personal struggle or crisis	6
Offer to join a post-church group	7
Change of geographical location	6
Offer to study – theology	1
Total	**40**

final factor that tipped the balance and acted as a turning point in their decision to leave the church (see Table 3.1).

What pastors said

An obvious source of information about why and how people leave would be church pastors and leaders. Suspecting that this would be the case I interviewed 54 church pastors, theologians, Christian counsellors and church consultants, many of whom were senior pastors in large EPC churches. As could be expected the range of reasons given by these EPC leaders was vast. Most were puzzled about why people left and at best offered only tentative explanations.

One pastor who had seen several people leave his church during the months prior to our conversation said, 'You can't do much about them. It is an awful thing to watch. But ultimately people have to decide for themselves, don't they.' Others clearly saw the leavers as 'backsliders', those who were giving up the faith. One spoke of Jesus' parable of the seed in different soils and said you had to expect some to fall away.

Perhaps the most blatant was a senior pastor of a large EPC church who I heard speak at a recent church leaders' conference. He suggested, to the crowd of over 300 church pastors and leaders, that every church needed a soundproof room where the pastor could take certain people and head-butt them. To make his point he acted out giving a 'Liverpool kiss' to an imaginary leaver. Of course, he added, this would be followed by prayer. The group of people he wanted to take into that room were the church leavers who left without saying a thing. He went on to say, 'My question is, "Were they ever part of the church?"' To justify his point he drew on the parable of the 'lost sheep' in which Jesus describes the good shepherd as the one who leaves the flock to search out the lost one. The pastor stated that the 'lost sheep' is not someone who knows where the paddock is and chooses to run away. We (pastors and leaders) shouldn't run after them, we are to stay with the crowd.

Such comments raise serious questions about the degree of awareness pastors and church leaders have of the concerns and issues faced by church leavers. To some degree this may be explained by a common factor in Ebaugh's leaving process which she calls 'mutual withdrawal'. This term describes the way that the church leaver and the church leadership pull back from each other. It is a process that

> involves both the individual's decreased association with a group and, simultaneously, the group's decreased demands on and involvement with the individual. As a group expects less from an individual, the rewards of belonging also decrease, such that withdrawal from the group becomes an increasingly viable option. (Ebaugh, 1988, p. 10)

Leavers spoke of a sense that not only were they withdrawing from the church but the church, especially leaders, were withdrawing from them at the same time. For example, where previously they would have been invited to leadership events or to be involved in ministry at the front of the church, many said that they were now subtly excluded.

Richter and Francis in their study of church leavers state that 'one of the most disconcerting findings from our questionnaire survey was that 92 per cent of leavers reported that no one from the church had talked with them about why they were attending less frequently, during the first six weeks after their church going dropped off' (Richter and Francis, 1998, p. 145).

Many of the pastors that I interviewed indicated that 'knockbacks' by the church, especially by key leaders, were the main reason people left the church. Conversely a significant number of interviewees spoke of such a 'knockback' not as the reason for their decision to leave but as the final factor in their overall decision. This indicates that pastors in the EPC churches have some feeling for the final factor that entices people to leave the church but not for the underlying process of leaving that the majority seem to go through. Their focus on this final (turning point) factor misses the underlying faith questions and disenchantment that appear to be part of people's journey out of the EPC church.

Often when I talk with church groups, questions are raised about the faith of leavers who walk away from the church – Are they walking away from the Christian faith as well? How committed were they? Did they have a good grounding in the faith to begin with? To answer these questions we need to look back at the people who are leaving. Ninety-four per cent of those I interviewed had held significant leadership positions within the church, 32 per cent had been full-time paid Christian workers for at least a year. A third had been to courses of study to strengthen and build their Christian faith. On average they had been involved in their respective churches, as adults, for 15.8 years. But perhaps most tellingly, during the interviews the vast majority spoke of very clear and vivid experiences of God at work in their lives.

Surprisingly, only one of the people I interviewed left with the intention of moving away from his Christian faith. The rest were clear that they were not choosing to leave their Christian faith when they left the church. As we will see in subsequent chapters, for many their leaving has led to a deepening of their faith. Many of the interviewees were aware that those within the church structures would see them as backsliding and they chose to comment about this during the interview:

Ruth I just think, don't turn round and tell me that I pulled out because I was backsliding. It is because of the spiritual side of me that I pulled out.

Delwyn I found that the disillusionment came with the church and how effective it is. And I came to a place of being so disillusioned that I began to question whether I was backsliding because of it. I had no real zeal any more for 'churchianity'. In fact lots of it so frustrated me that I just found it difficult even to go. So the whole question came – had I 'backslidden'? – it wasn't until we met with others of like mind that I began to realize that it was not the case. There are other people out there who feel exactly as I do. Then the whole condemnation of 'backsliddenness' began to leave me. And I began to feel there had to be answers for the church of the 1990s.

We've not advanced at all. We are still doing exactly the same things as we did decades ago. And little wonder that we are not effective.

Jim It's not that I've backslidden over the last four years. Well, hey, I've been trained and I'm highly equipped and I've been working out in the community over the last four years, and just meeting some people and just doing some good things. And I mightn't have my little badge from the Sunday meeting, but I've come to the realization that's totally unimportant.

Tim I had to give it up [my church] for the sake of theology. I could have kept all our networks but our theology changed. I don't think we could have stayed in our Baptist church thinking what we do. That's obvious so we had to leave. We felt exiled, really banished by shame and a change of theology and a sense that – you know – that we were no longer stage two, we were stage three believers. And it is very sad. To have people think that you have 'backslidden' and in fact you have done quite the reverse. So there is still a very big hole in my heart and a lot of sadness really. Just like if I had a kid that grew up and died before they had lived out their life I would still be sad and I'm still sad about having to leave our church. I'm sad about that.

The disparity between the views of church leaders who were either puzzled, tentative or blaming the individual, and the comments of church leavers themselves, points to the lack of communication between the two. Very few church leaders talked of incidents where they had sat down with leavers from their own churches, or any other church, to hear people's reasons and learn from them. This sideline speculation of the leaders continued despite their knowledge that many of the leavers were intelligent, creative and innovative people who had previously been significant leaders within their churches.

When church leaders did give reasons they focused on the increased pressure on people's time with new leisure opportunities, TV, work demands, and growing numbers of women in the workforce. Such societal changes were seen as increasing the pressures on people and decreasing their discretionary time. While the leavers too identified these pressures only 10 per cent indicated that they were a factor in their decision to leave and of those this was a relatively minor contributing factor in their final decision. As we will see later, the majority of leavers move to post-church groups to nurture their faith after leaving, and these too demand time and commitment.

A common theme from the interviews with church leaders is the focus on the church structure and church leadership as a reason people leave. As one pastor said, 'It is usually out of deep disappointment and disillusionment with leadership, either leadership decisions or poor counselling.' For 18 per cent of the leavers these factors were the predominant reasons given for leaving. However, for the remaining 82 per cent such disillusionment may have been a factor but not a critical one.

One aspect of leadership disillusionment that was mentioned regularly by pastors and ministers was a number of situations where church leaders had 'fallen' and subsequently disillusioned large numbers of people. This is where pastors were found to be involved in adulterous relationships and/or financial impropriety. There appeared to be a general understanding that where significant leaders 'fell' in this way there was a high degree of disillusionment and subsequent leaving of the church. Although I interviewed a number of leavers who had been involved in churches where the senior pastor had 'fallen' in some spectacular fashion, no one identified this as a major factor in their decision to leave. Such events undoubtedly caused disillusionment with that pastor and often pastors in general. It also motivated a number of interviewees to move from one church to another, and may have been a factor in their decision to leave church altogether. But no one identified this as the principal or sole reason for their leaving the church. On the contrary, many discussed the disappointment of being deceived by a leader as a situation through which their faith in God had strengthened and matured as they learned to be less dependent on church leaders. A more important factor in their decision to stay or leave the church was based on how the leadership elected to handle the difficulty. Where it was hidden, swept under the carpet or not openly dealt with people lost a greater degree of confidence in the leadership.

Within the group of 54 church leaders interviewed were ten theological lecturers and four Christian counsellors and psychotherapists. A very small number of the pastors but the vast majority of lecturers and counsellors raised another reason for people's decisions to leave: the changing dynamic of people's faith which often encourages them to move outside of the church. This was a reason which meshed with the accounts of leavers.

What struck me was the depth of understanding of many of the lecturers, all of the counsellors but only a very small number of the pastors and ministers about the changing faith dynamics at work within leavers. One of the most disturbing results of the research is the sense that the majority of those leading and pastoring in EPC churches are ignorant of the crucial reasons why people leave the church. Their ignorance remains despite the detailed knowledge of lecturers in theological colleges, counsellors and a number of leavers who have well-articulated and comprehensive understandings of the changing faith dynamics that lead people to leave the EPC church.

In the next four chapters we will meet four major groups of EPC church leavers and discover the background to why they left and also consider their faith outside the EPC church.

FOUR

Disillusioned followers

The timing of my first interview with Keith and Laura Brown coincided with the end of Keith's work day. As I walked up the drive of their detached house in Kingston, Keith was finishing up with his last client for the day, while Laura tidied the work area ready for the next morning. Laura and Keith Brown are a married couple in their early forties with two children. Keith runs a business from home that allows him and Laura to make a comfortable income. As we initially talked over a cup of coffee, they both spoke with enthusiasm about their part in the research and their impression that what I was studying was really important for 'the church at large'.

With the tape recorder running, Laura and Keith launched straight into their reasons for leaving the church and the pain they experienced in doing so. When we talked they had been out of the church for a year and a half. They spoke of being heavily involved in a local charismatic church. They had become Christians during a period of separation in their marriage and subsequently joined the church that they were a part of for 16 years. They explained that they saw their 'newfound' Christian faith as the reason their marriage got back together – it was a chance to start again on a new footing. As a result they had very excitedly become involved in the church. Soon Laura's brother Steve and his wife Gwyn became Christians and joined the same church where they too were actively involved.

For the Browns, church became a large part of their lives. They became part of the church leadership, leading home groups, prayer groups, and being called on to 'minister' during ministry times at the church.[1] When their church began to take on a new direction (the Toronto Blessing[2]) the Browns embraced it and were fully supportive of the changes. Their pastors, like many others at the time, wished to change the activities of the church to include more and more of this new 'blessing'. The change of direction was eventually seen by Keith and Laura as being contrary to what they believed God wanted to do within their church. Keith saw the introduction of this new focus as a man-made phenomenon rather than something from God. Laura saw it as evil.

Keith We've seen with our own eyes a progression of people beginning to idolize and worship men. Their eyes have been moved off God to the eloquence, to the charismatic gifts. I'm not talking spiritual gifts, I'm talking natural charismatic gifts of men and of women and of leaders, with brilliant oratory skill and humour. They manipulate, induce, suck in and abuse people. I am longing for the day when men of God will stand up in the true mantle of prophets and say, 'That is not God. Sit down and shut up!'

Laura We actually began to have physical symptoms. We would come home and we would feel physically ill. And we'd be driving off to church and feeling ill, and when you'd get into the building you'd just have a physical reaction. I particularly tried to overcome it, because I was determined I wasn't going to leave my church family. I've been with them for the last 15, no, 16 years and these are my friends. I thought, 'No, it's my problem. I'm going along with this if it's the last thing I do.'

Increasingly, the Browns came to see that it wasn't an issue where they needed to change, it was the church that was heading down the wrong track.

Keith We realized that what we had been reading in the Word of God was coming into conflict with what we were hearing. It was hell in many ways – this internal conflict and torment at times, mental anguish going on. Trying to think what we were sensing in our spirit was in conflict with what we were hearing.

The shift in focus of attention off themselves and onto the church was not an easy one and meant a lot of confusion before they developed confidence in their own viewpoint. Eventually Laura and Keith came to interpret the new move of the church as something not from God but from the devil.

Laura We believe that what is happening here is witchcraft. Wherever there's domination, intimidation, control of this kind it's witchcraft. That's a very unpopular thing to say. And with that a scripture in Revelation became very, very meaningful to us. Revelation 2.20 says that those who tolerate Jezebel, those who commit adultery with her, will be cast upon a bed of suffering and affliction. I still believe that to this day.

Convinced that their church was heading into error the Browns wrote to, met and discussed their concerns with the elders of the church and the pastor. After repeated attempts to rescue the church from its involvement and, in their minds, total capitulation to this new 'move', they began to become disillusioned. The Browns, who were always in the front row at their church, began to sit further to the back on Sunday mornings. Whereas before they were actively participating in the service 'ministry times', they now began to hang back and watch. Initially they only observed but as the months went by they started to show their disgust with what was going on at the front.

> *Laura* So often people would be told, 'Now we will pray in tongues. Now everybody will come up the front. Now we will do this, now we will do that.' And we'd be standing in the back row on our own, looking around and everyone else would be joining in. Well, it becomes very obvious in the end that you are not flowing with everyone else. This happened time and time again.
>
> *Keith* We'd be left standing on our own.
>
> *Laura* Because we couldn't do it. We just couldn't do it.

In response the leadership began to question their actions, accusing them of 'bad body language', of not being a part of the new move of God and 'resisting the Spirit'. The Browns found they were no longer asked to be involved in 'ministry' in the services or in other leadership positions within the church as they had been previously. People who would have been referred to them for prayer were now encouraged to go to others. Not long after this the Browns were formally asked by the church leadership not to pray with people in the church.

Finally, after months of going to church reluctantly and with a growing feeling of disgust for what the church was becoming, the Browns left. They were angry that the church couldn't see what they saw – that God was not a part of this new 'Toronto Blessing'. Angry and confused, they began to practise their Christian faith outside the church.

The Browns and leavers like them become disillusioned with the church. During their time in EPC churches they have accepted or formed an expectation of what the church will be, how it will function and what its goals, practices and processes should be like. This expectation or illusion of the church has been severely undermined by the practice of a particular church or their experience of churches in general. This disillusionment is not normally the result of some relatively minor incident or issue.

The Browns are part of a group I came to call 'angry' leavers. Although the 'angry' leavers leave because of a whole variety of specific issues, they are all angry about a major church decision, direction, leadership structure or with a key church leader. Typically they base the 'incorrectness' of the church's decisions on what they understand of Scripture. Keith constantly referred to Scripture as the basis of his decision to leave:

> *Keith* The thing that really began to concern me was the fact that we began more and more to move experientially, rather than on the book, and the validity of the Word of God. And so I began to have problems internally. I kept thinking 'This is wrong because what is actually being said is not adding up with the Word of God.' But because those in positions of power and authority in the institution were directing traffic, and telling people this is God, this is God doing this, this is God doing that, incredible layers of claptrap were going down.
>
> And then what happens is there seems to be no voice, or voices, saying, 'Hang on a minute, let's weigh this thing up.' The Bible says if somebody prophesies let the other prophets test it and weigh it up.[3]

For other 'angry' leavers, the focus of their disillusionment is on other areas of church life. For one couple, Christine and Roger, it was the dictatorial way in which the pastor was seen to control their church. Whatever the issue for this category of leavers, anger at the direction and leadership of the church is the common linking factor. Anger, though, is not the only emotion felt. Many also feel betrayed and find their leaving very difficult. Their church has been highly significant to them and the decision to leave is therefore very traumatic. The pain of this is accentuated because they believe the church has in some significant way not only betrayed them, but also the gospel, the heart of the Christian faith.

> *Christine* It was very traumatic for both of us. Particularly so for Roger, having been involved in his home church all his life. He has grown up in that church. And that particular church has supported us in mission ever since. We had to come to the decision to say enough is enough – we are out.

A number of disillusioned leavers don't leave angry, but through a sense of disappointment and hurt with their church. They have accepted an understanding of how the church will care for and respond to people in need, but didn't receive this level of support when they most needed it. As a result they leave disillusioned. Often these leavers had an impression of the church as a 'family' or caring community that could be relied on to be there when you really needed them.

For two of the leavers this disillusionment was experienced as they worked through a marital separation and the resultant responsibility for the children and getting an income, as well as the emotional pain of being stigmatized as a separated person within the church. For a married couple, it was the cumulative pain of serious illness, severely rebellious teenagers, depression and resultant loneliness.

The title Disillusioned Followers indicates that these 'angry' and 'hurt' leavers have left the church because of specific grumbles about the direction, leadership or level of care offered by the church. But these specific

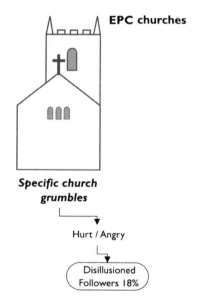

Figure 4.1 Journeys of faith outside of the EPC church
Trajectory 1 – Disillusioned Followers

grumbles have not led them to question the 'taken-for-granteds' of the EPC faith that they received from the church. Hence their Christian faith outside the church remains largely the same as the faith they held to during their time in the church. For many this faith is held to even more tightly and with higher degrees of commitment than in their church days.

The Disillusioned Followers made up 17.5 per cent of those interviewed.[4] On average they had been participating adult members[5] of their respective churches for 13.5 years and had been outside the church (i.e. the time since they had left) for 3.5 years when I interviewed them. Two of the Disillusioned Followers grew up in an EPC church. The remaining seventeen had made adult decisions to join an EPC church. For nine there had been some childhood involvement in a 'mainstream' church prior to their decision to join an EPC church. The remaining eight had no childhood church involvement. In order to describe their faith I want to look at four characteristics of their post-church faith.

A received faith

Disillusioned Followers
Received faith

Although the Disillusioned Followers have disengaged from the church, they have not disengaged from an EPC faith. In fact for many, particularly the 'angry' leavers, part of their claim is that they, unlike the church they left, have remained true to the evangelical/Pentecostal/charismatic faith.

Their faith is characterized as 'received' because it is the faith that they received when they entered the church. The Disillusioned Followers had been through a process of conversion and accepted the Christian faith as truth. This faith is something they received as a complete package as they entered the church community. Here people had very strong and deeply-held beliefs, but when asked to outline the basis for these beliefs they inevitably refer to an unquestioned acceptance of some external authority source. In the case of the people I interviewed, this reference point was usually their more literalistic interpretation of a passage of

Scripture or the teaching of some respected Christian leader. Such beliefs tend to be dualistic, with clear divisions between what is true and untrue, right and wrong, good and bad.

A dependent relationship

Disillusioned Followers
Received faith **Dependent relationship**

Although the Disillusioned Followers have left a particular church and are therefore not at church on Sundays, they nevertheless continue to be dependent on the wider EPC community. Because they no longer receive the teaching and support for their faith in a church setting they now have to find this from other sources. A whole variety of these are available and were used by Disillusioned Followers, including listening to Christian radio or watching Christian TV programmes, attending non-church-based seminars and workshops, and reading Christian books and magazines. Rebecca and Murray put it this way:

Rebecca Well, we have Premier Radio[6] on regularly, all day.

Murray That certainly helps, yeah.

Rebecca We tape the preaching on TV that comes on in the mornings.

Interviewer And you would listen to them at some point?

Rebecca Oh yes.

Hamish, who had no connection with Murray and Rebecca, said:

Hamish I like listening to radio preachers. It's a good way to start your day by having a dose of them and then going off to work!

While the Disillusioned Followers have left the EPC church, in the sense of leaving a church that meets in particular buildings on a Sunday morning, or membership of a particular church body, their faith nevertheless remains closely connected to and dependent on the wider EPC community. One interviewee talked of joining Promise Keepers[7] and really loving it. Others attend specific seminars led by Christian speakers, or prophetic ministry seminars. One talked of a network of ex-Pentecostal churchgoers around the country that met together occasionally. Four of the Disillusioned Followers who had been part of the same church talked of joining together with a number of others once a fortnight for a house church gathering. As Laura's brother Steve says:

> *Steve* I think the fellowship aspect with other Christians is very important. That phrase that the Bible uses about iron sharpening iron; we hone each other for refining, and we can encourage each other in the faith. That would be a key thing for people who leave the church system, to maintain some sort of fellowship network. Whether that be formal, or informal is up to the people, I guess.

While the Disillusioned Followers remain dependent on the wider EPC community they also adhere to the personal faith practices of the EPC church. Part of the evangelical emphasis has been on the personal practices of prayer, Bible reading, financial giving and service to others and God's work in the world. The Disillusioned Followers typically continue on in these personal practices.

> *Anne-Marie* A friend gave me a good Bible, which I read, and I always watch *Songs of Praise* on TV. I've kept some really good hymn books. And a lot of singing, often songs do come to me when I need help or I'm out on my own, but can still have the 'worshippy' spiritual thing. I do a lot of walks and I often walk and sing. I take my song book to the bath before the kids get up and have a good old half an hour. I'm always up before the kids get up – I get up a good half to three-quarters of an hour before them and have a quiet time. I read the Bible. It's a time alone. I also maintain contact with the people I know who are Christians.

For these Disillusioned Followers, whether the Bible is read regularly or irregularly it is always approached in a relatively uncritical fashion. The attitude is one which says, 'Here is the word of God; if I read it God will speak to me or guide me.' Prayer is equally engaged in the same form as they used to pray in their church. However, most mention that it is harder to give time to prayer without the external encouragement of the church community with its prayer meetings and reminders of the importance of prayer. In this way, these leavers often experience a sense of guilt that they are not carrying on their prayer lives as they feel they 'should'.

In interviewing these leavers about their Christian practices, 'should' was a significant word. They accepted uncritically the expectations of EPC Christians to spend time in prayer, reading the Bible, meeting with and serving others. A number were not holding to this sense of 'should' and in that way felt they were doing less than what they would expect of themselves. What is important to note is the acceptance of the 'shoulds' if not the continuation of the practices themselves.

> *Gwyn* I would have to admit I don't pray, and I don't read as much perhaps as when I was in a church situation. And some of that would be because the responsibilities and positions I've held within the church system necessitated me pushing that much harder. So there's a slackening off, if you like. But in there, there is that core, that thread that remains.

The Disillusioned Follower's faith therefore remains a dependent faith both on the wider EPC community and the personal devotional practices at the heart of evangelicalism.

An unexamined faith

Disillusioned Followers
Received faith
Dependent relationship
Unexamined faith

The specific grumbles the Disillusioned Followers have with their church, or churches in general, have not driven them to re-examine the 'taken-for-granteds' of the EPC faith, as Amanda and Anne-Marie explain.

> *Amanda* In the end I adopted the attitude of 'We've not lost faith, but become critical of the people in the church.' I felt that if you are a Christian I had the right to expect to see some form of Christ-likeness in you. And I thought, these are people who don't even know the basic parts of God's word. I became disappointed in my expectations of a Christian brother or sister.

> *Anne-Marie* But you don't lose your faith. I didn't. You cling to certain verses like Romans 8, which says 'Who can separate us from the love of Christ?' I thought church is not whether I go to a building. That was the revelation when I became a Christian; it's not going to Sunday Mass[8] each week. It's

taking it all on board. So not feeling settled in one particular church isn't going to take your faith away.

For this group the taken-for-granteds of the EPC faith are reinforced through an external trusted authority. The most common of these reference points was an unquestioning reading of the Scriptures. The second involved trusting the word or advice of a key Christian leader who they felt they could rely on. Typically, these key Christian leaders included writers, prophets and teachers, with the most common being a previous pastor. For some the teaching, lifestyle or advice of a key Christian leader or leaders has become an internalized inner voice which they continue to trust. Another external authority source involved reference to a personal dream, vision or prophecy.[9]

Typically, however, it is a combination of these authorities which is referred to as the basis for the taken-for-granteds of their faith with their interpretation of the Bible being the final arbiter of all decisions regarding what is true. In this way they express a faith that is reliant on an unexamined authority.

For the Disillusioned Followers the journey out of the church has not seriously shaken the core aspects of the EPC faith they received in the church. Their external authority base – whether it be Scripture, reference to dreams or prophecy or their own internal reference point – provides a basis for what is right and wrong, good practice and bad practice for Christians. Because the foundations, the core beliefs and values of the Disillusioned Followers' faith remain, intact they therefore have a solid foundation of faith from which to speak and act.

A bold faith

Disillusioned Followers
Received faith
Dependent relationship
Unexamined faith
Bold

As I got up to leave that night Keith suggested that they pray for me and my research. We stood by the dining room table and bowed our heads as he began to pray a long and fervent prayer that God would work through what I was doing and help to bring the church around to seeing its error. He prayed for the Spirit's protection on me and my family as I did this work, as there would be opposition and 'the enemy'[10] would be sure to want to interfere. After responding in prayer for them I walked back out into the cold, damp night somewhat dazed by their passion both for their faith and against the church.

For Keith and Laura and other Disillusioned Followers, their Christian faith remained very important to them. While their specific grumbles have led them to question their church or churches in general, it has not led them to question the core elements of the faith they received from the EPC church. As Keith said to me, 'There was never any doubt as far as shipwrecking our relationship with the Lord Jesus. That was never an issue.'

Disillusioned Followers remain strongly committed to their faith. Their faith is described as bold because they remain sure, confident and bold in their explanation of both their faith and their decision to leave the church. They express a certainty in their decision and present understandings of faith not found in the leavers we will meet in the next chapter.

Looking to the future

The 'hurt' and 'angry' Disillusioned Followers view their future relationship with the church differently. The 'hurts' are far more open to returning to church in the future, although the risk of being hurt again often holds them back.

> *Tracey* I have been thinking I would love to go again, but it'd be back to being hurt again – because it is a form of hurting. And I'm quite happy in my four little walls, thank you very much. I don't know that I want to step out, and open myself up. But equally there is the yearning to go. My youngest daughter is very involved with church. We have been all over the place in our family. And she has sort of been at me and at me and at me, and sort of saying, 'Why don't you go, why don't you go?' and I've been, I went to her baptism a few weeks ago. But that service – I couldn't take it, it was so dry.

If they do move back into a church they will be looking for one that would be more accepting and caring of the people within it.

> *Grant* There's a bit of hope on the horizon. But I said to Amanda [his wife] really, when I look at church and the reason for it I would be very, very skeptical about going back. I don't want that hurt. I don't ever want to expose myself in that way. Pouring myself out and having to face that hurt, that disappointment – I just couldn't do that. I'm not anti-God, I still believe in all the principles. I believe in the love of God. It'd take a lot of things now to get me back involved in church life.

The 'angry' leavers, not surprisingly, tend to view their future involvement in a church with less optimism. For them the reason they left church was because they saw the church heading off in a 'wrong direction' and they are therefore very reluctant about returning to an institutional church. As Keith says:

> *Keith* Yeah, I want to walk with Jesus. And to do the best that I can. He [Jesus] spent 99 per cent of his time outside the temple of the Pharisees. He did a bit of teaching in the temple. But most of his life was spent outside of there. Most of the disciples were outside there.
>
> But also I can't see anywhere in Scripture, particularly from Matthew through Revelation, where there is something that is some discernible, biblically based outline of what we've currently got in the way of the institution [church]. I can't see that it bears any resemblance to it. For the life of me, I've tried. I've tried and tried and tried and said, 'Well, you know, what the institutions do, where does it appear in here?' And to that which can be proved to bear, I'm holding fast. That's what I'm desiring to do.

Again, Keith's reluctance to rejoin the church is based on his understanding of the Bible, and in this case the way the church as he knew it was functioning outside of his interpretation of the Bible. Other Disillusioned Followers are equally clear that the form of the church they left is not something they wish to return to, but they will be guided by what God wants rather than their own personal view. For many there was an expectation that God is in the process of starting something different, and a new form of church will emerge in the future of which they will be a part. As Laura's brother Steve and his wife Gwyn said:

Gwyn I wait for direction from God. I'm not going out looking for anything. I am looking for him to direct me for what he wants me to do. I want to know him more deeply still. I want to go on. I've got to the point where I'll do anything that he asks me. You know, if he asks me to move out of this house then I will do it. I think that he will bring other Christians along across our path that we'll be joined up with. And he'll supernaturally do it.

Steve For me, I personally can't see myself going back into the church system as it exists now. And I firmly believe the church will not exist in its current form in years to come, the main reason being that it's strayed from the baseline that God's set. And the purposes that he's called Christians to. That's where we see our future. Individually I'm believing we'll be a part of that, this new church of God.

For some of the Disillusioned Followers there were indications of another set of grumbles beginning to emerge after they left the church. One person, who had been out of the church for 12 years, commented that he is now less satisfied with the faith diet that he receives from sources that were originally inspiring and nurturing his faith.

Andrew For years I've actually really enjoyed listening to the Premier Radio programmes but there are times I just do not want to hear some of the teaching, simply because I feel as if I'm coming under that 'you ought to be' kind of thing. There are times when maybe I'm visiting with my father-in-law, who's a retired Pentecostal pastor, or I'm reading some of the books that Dad reads, and I feel the old kinds of pressures and expectations to be doing this or to be doing that. And I kind of think it's just not where I'm at, and I just kind of turn off and it's again a whole set of expectations that I'm expected to live up to and it's just not where the Lord's taken me.

Here there are indications of wanting to look beyond the ought-to-bes, and the shoulds of the EPC faith. As another person said, 'I have a lot of questions and there are a lot of things that I have changed my thinking on. I used to believe blindly what the preacher was saying. I believed blindly what everyone was saying but I think I question more now.' This can be seen as a move to a deeper examination of faith – its beliefs, values and expectations. Here the comments of the interviewees reflect a dissatisfaction that is broader and less clearly articulated than those generally expressed by the Disillusioned Followers.

NOTES

1 Ministry times refer to the term used within EPC churches for the time in or immediately after a service when people can ask others to pray for them. In this particular church, as is the practice within many churches, there were specific people authorized to pray for those seeking prayer in the 'ministry times'.

2 The Toronto Blessing began at the Airport Vineyard Church in Toronto where it was reported during 1994 that a new 'visitation' of God had been occurring. This 'visitation' was later named the 'Toronto Blessing' by the British Press (Anderson, 1995, p. 7). The 'visitation' has been experienced by six or seven thousand visitors a week for over three years (1994–7) as visitors from all over the world visit to 'catch the fire'. Many pastors and church leaders have visited the Vineyard Church for this purpose, many attempting to bring 'the blessing' back to their own churches. The importation of this blessing within churches has created debate and some division as church leaders and attenders differ as to whether this 'visitation' is of God.

3 Here Keith refers to 1 Corinthians 14.29, which states 'Two or three prophets should speak, and the others should weigh carefully what is said.'

4 Nineteen of those interviewed.

5 Eighteen years of age or over.

6 A Christian radio station.

7 Promise Keepers is an evangelical Christian men's movement which began in the United States. The movement is described in its own promotional material in the following way: 'Promise Keepers is a Christ-centred ministry, dedicated to uniting men through vital relationships to become godly influences in their world.'

8 Anne-Marie was brought up in a Catholic church prior to choosing to join an EPC church. This reference is to her previous Catholic church involvement where Mass attendance was considered important in the same way EPC churches encourage participants to be regular attenders at church services.

9 What may be called within the EPC churches a 'witness of the Spirit,' which is an inner 'feeling', 'intuition' or 'understanding'. The source of such an 'inner witness' is perceived by the person as being beyond their own 'feelings', 'intuitions' and 'understandings'. Rather they see the source of this 'understanding' as being from the Holy Spirit.

10 Here he was using a common word to imply the 'devil' or 'Satan'.

FIVE

Reflective exiles

My dominant image of Jane, who we met in Chapter 3, is of a highly motivated and intelligent woman. When I interviewed her, Jane was in her final year of a psychology degree; her study had to be fitted around a full-time job in a government department, bringing up two children as a solo mum and her work with a voluntary medical association, as well as the flower and cleaning rosters at her local church. It is these rosters that remain her final link with the church. In fact, she hasn't been to a service for over two years and only went very infrequently the year before that. She only continues with the rosters because it is a very small traditional church, with a lot of elderly people, and if she didn't do it she is not sure who would. It is a long way from her days as a pastor's wife in a thriving Pentecostal church with over a thousand people at the main service.

Jane raises her hands to gesture the speech marks around the word 'Christians' as she explains how she first became involved in the church. It was 1973 and Jane, then in her late teens, was invited to a Pentecostal church in Harrogate by a friend.

> *Jane* I was at a bit of a crisis period. I came from a very dysfunctional family and the people at the church were very friendly, very hospitable and I certainly could sense something there. There was a certain atmosphere or presence, and I think because I was quite needy at the time, it was sort of like a ready-made answer. Christians had some solution for everything. I didn't need to work anything out any more. It was like a package deal and all the answers were there. No more questions about the meaning of life.

Jane was from then on involved, as she puts it, 'lock, stock and barrel' in all the activities of her church. Undoubtedly the church helped her: 'It gave me a sense of identity, and for the first few years it was really good for me, because it helped me sort out a lot of things from my past – it was a very positive experience.' After a few years she moved to Leeds, and a much bigger Pentecostal church where she married one of the key leaders who would become a pastoral staff member of one of the largest Pentecostal churches in the UK.

For Jane, the period of being heavily involved began to come to an end. Despite her best efforts to remain actively involved, it became more and more difficult for her to be there.

> *Jane* I tried to be involved, I had a continual battle, I was starting to question a lot of the basic philosophies . . . I don't know where I am as far as believing in God, or who Jesus was and things like that. I'm not sure about that now, but I don't sort of feel I have to know that. But I think there is a lot of wisdom in the Bible that stands on its own. It has a lot of good principles to live by.

It is this questioning of the basic beliefs of the EPC faith that distinguishes Jane and others like her from the Disillusioned Followers discussed in the previous chapter. The leavers we will meet in this chapter have grumbles that question the foundations of the EPC faith they had previously believed. They are grumbles directed at the meta-narratives (overarching accounts) provided by the EPC church. They are not grumbles about specifics within the church but about the function, role and place of church itself. Grumbles about what it means to be a Christian. How much are we left to do our own thing in life? What is prayer? How do we understand and use the Bible? Even, Who is Jesus? and for some, Does God exist? To distinguish these foundational grumbles from the specific church practice grumbles of the Disillusioned Followers I have called them 'meta-grumbles'.[1] Meta-grumbles question the deep-rooted foundations of the faith itself. The people described here are reflecting on and questioning the basis of the Christian faith received from the EPC church community. For these people it is the core of their faith that is being shaken in this process.

> *Rosemary* We are not really maintaining our faith. Our problem is not so much with the church, but it is with God as well.

> *Fiona* It seems like things have come down to the basics of who am I and who is God *and* I don't know if I am anywhere near finding out. But it seems a lot more clear, in that the church and all that stuff isn't there. If God is going to speak to me, he will have to do it in a way that is not sort of linked

to anything. So there is sort of a freshness there, in a way, and a sense of not being bound to what we were used to.

People like Jane, whom I have labelled the Reflective Exiles, are not leaving the church because it is not functioning as it should, or because they have relational difficulties with the leaders or disapprove of the new vision or direction of the church, but because of a more foundational questioning of their underlying faith. The 'specific grumbles' relating to church structure and leadership may all be factors in bringing people to the point of questioning the core beliefs and values of the EPC community of which their church or para-church is a part. These core beliefs, values and expected behaviours are part of the taken-for-granted elements of the church community. To question these is to potentially undermine the core foundations of the community itself.

Often what stimulates people to begin such questioning can be specific grumbles with the church, but they can also be sparked and fuelled by a variety of other events. These include personal crises and changes such as major health, employment and relational or marital status changes and exposure to alternative meta-narratives. Common alternative meta-narratives encountered by people were highlighted through personal study (e.g. feminist studies at university), a work environment, or significant friendships. In the accounts of many of the people I interviewed it was a combination of a number of such factors that nudged them to consider in new ways the basis and core of their faith. Whatever the combination of factors, in each case they gave the individual a reference point outside of the traditional authorities from which to reflect and question their previously accepted EPC beliefs and faith package.

Disillusioned Followers (of Chapter 4) may have been exposed to the same kinds of disruptions to the faith, but unlike this new group, Reflective Exiles, they did not go on to question the core foundations of their faith. In this way the Reflective Exiles are in a quite different faith position from the Disillusioned Followers.

> *Angela* It's so difficult to look at your own life and what you really do believe in, the nitty-gritty, when you're constantly trying to put forward a certain persona for other people. It's very difficult to be honest sometimes in front of other people and I just got to a stage where I acknowledged that I wasn't

being an honest person. It's been a really good opportunity to just say, 'Well, what do I believe?' And yeah, doing a bit of extra reading, not just from the Bible, but looking at other material. Oh, certainly not other religions but more just a general holistic look at life, where do we fit into the scheme of things? So it's been really quite interesting. Certainly looked at a lot of different areas. Personal growth, healing and things like that. Last year my mother got really sick and that was a time that we were able to look at the meaning of life in a very deep way, reassess things. You just change your priorities and you take stock of things.

Angela's comments reflect the desire of leavers like her to question and examine the core foundations of their faith. This process of questioning begins while they are still part of the church and extends throughout the leaving process, and for many well after they left. Although dealing with similar questions, doubts and issues, Angela and Jane have related differently to their church as they worked through their questions. Angela left the church relatively early on in this process as she slowly withdrew over 18 months. Jane, on the other hand, remained tied to the church not by choice but through her husband's involvement and his career as a pastor. For Jane, it was to be ten years from the time these doubts and questions began to emerge and she found herself mentally withdrawing until she was finally able to leave completely. For Jane these ten years were a very disturbing and difficult period in her life. She could see much of the good that the church was doing and yet felt that it was becoming constricting on who she wanted to be as a person. Her journey out has similarities with the Disillusioned Followers discussed in the previous chapter but differs sharply in the level of her questioning.

The fact that a number of Disillusioned Followers who were interviewed gave indications that since leaving the church the focus of their questions and doubts was shifting in the direction of critically reassessing the foundational beliefs, values and behaviours of the EPC church community indicates that people can move from the faith position represented as Disillusioned Follower towards that of the Reflective Exiles. This is suggested in Figure 5.1 by the dotted line between Disillusioned Followers and Reflective Exiles.

When I talked with Jane she was quite clear that she hadn't lost her faith. This was a common comment among the Reflective Exiles. Although

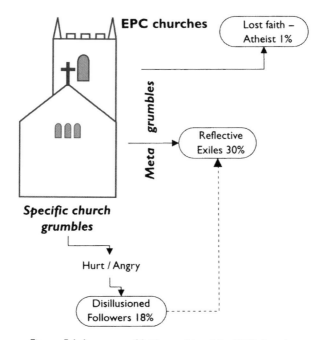

Figure 5.1 Journeys of faith outside of the EPC church
Trajectory 2 – Reflective Exiles

Jane was concerned to make sure I knew she hadn't lost her faith, it was difficult to grasp what Jane's faith involved or how it affected her life now. When the Reflective Exiles talked about their present faith they were often quite confused and many questions about the details of their faith were, as Jane's conversation illustrates, answered with an 'I don't know'.

Interviewer Would you characterize yourself as having a continued spirituality and faith?

Jane Definitely [*said immediately and emphatically*].

Interviewer Would you characterize that as having a Christian flavour?

Jane Um, probably, more from sort of habit and because I know a lot about Christianity and it's really familiar territory for me. I've spent thousands of hours in Bible studies and stuff. So to a certain extent that is just a familiar groove. But for quite a few years I couldn't think about it, I just couldn't. I don't read the Bible. But I know a lot of it. And it sort of comes to me from time to time in certain situations.

The same sort of responses came through in an interview with Melissa:

Interviewer So faith for you still has a Christian flavour.

Melissa [hesitates] Um . . .

Interviewer Things like prayer and the Bible: do they have any place for you now?

Melissa I would really like to say yes it does, and I would love to have something really that is a bit more tangible than what I've got, but like I said before, all that stuff still clouds my thinking and I just need to get rid of a lot of the crap that I was left with. But careful too that you don't throw the baby out with the bath water. Because I still do believe in certain things. And I'd love to one day just start afresh and without all the shit.

The label Reflective Exiles is drawn from the dominant characteristic of such leavers – their reflective disposition towards the church they had belonged to, the faith they had received and their future faith direction. The term 'exile' must on first impression seem a curious label to be used of people who choose to leave the church, when a strict definition of 'exile' implies a form of enforced banishment. However, drawing on the work of Veling, 'exile' too can be an option. Veling says:

In what way is exile an option, something chosen? Generally speaking, I think it is true that we are more inclined to stay close to all that has gone before us because it is not an easy thing to depart – to take leave of 'all that to which we belong.' It is not easy to think a new thing; harder still to live in a condition of exile. Yet sometimes that is what it takes to escape the binding of a book [the expression he uses for a tradition or religious belief and belonging] that no longer holds as it used to. Particularly in the face of dominant institutions and orderings of reality that cling to the safety of the same, there are times that urge us to depart, times when we feel we must take up the nomadic existence of an exiled wanderer, in order to enlarge and set free the home to which we belong – the place we never really leave. (Veling, 1996, p. 78)

It is in the sense implied by Veling that exile is seen as an option chosen by EPC church leavers. The word 'exile' also encapsulates the feelings of those who have left. The feeling of being an 'outsider' from one's home-land, one's place of belonging. Hannah Ward and Jennifer Wild, speaking of women leaving churches in the United Kingdom, state that:

> In the experience of many contemporary Christians there is a real sense of wilderness, a sense of having grown out of or away from, old belief systems and forms of worship. We experience the present as barren and bewildering. The old has died but the new is beyond our grasp. (Ward and Wild, 1995, p. 3)

This is the experience of the Reflective Exiles.

Counter-dependency

Disillusioned Followers	Reflective Exiles
Dependent relationship	**Counter-dependent relationship[2]**

The Disillusioned Followers discussed in Chapter 4 had disengaged from active participation in a church but remained dependent upon the wider EPC church community through reading books and magazines, watching Christian TV shows, listening to radio preachers and music or attending seminars and workshops. They had also continued in the personal faith practices of the EPC church, such as personal times of prayer and Bible reading, financial giving and service to others as well as searching out fellowship with like-minded people. In this sense, the faith of these leavers was still nurtured by and dependent upon the wider EPC community and this community's personal devotional practices.

Unlike the Disillusioned Followers, Jane, and other Reflective Exiles, developed a counter-dependent attitude towards the whole EPC com-munity. Jane did not find her faith nurtured by listening to Christian radio shows, or watching Christian TV. She did not read Christian books or attend seminars. In fact, if people like Jane talked about these media at all, they talked about them as something with which they would have nothing to do. When I asked this category of leavers what nurtured their faith now, many answered, 'Well, it is certainly not . . .'

This answer exemplifies the counter-dependent relationship they have with the EPC community. For a number of the Reflective Exiles this opposition extended to a distinct dislike of anything that reminded them of the EPC church community they had left.

This counter-dependent[3] stage emerges as the person begins to question the taken-for-granted nature of the faith community's beliefs, values and expected behaviours. Sharon Parks' model of adult faith development from which the term 'counter-dependency' is drawn states:

> A person's feelings will continue to be shaped by this assumed authority until the day when there is the yearning (or absolute necessity) to explore and test oneself. This may occur in the midst of the utter shipwreck of the truth one has depended upon (in which case it may be accompanied by feelings of devastation, betrayal, bewilderment or the like), or it may emerge as a manifestation of just a restlessness arising as a sort of readiness for more being. In the latter instance, it is as though a strength has been established which can now 'push away from the dock' of what has been sure moorage, to move out into the deep waters of exploring for oneself what is true and trustworthy. Initially, however, this move is essentially another form of dependence, since this pushing away from the dock takes the form of counter-dependence . . . counter-dependence is the move in opposition to authority, that provides momentum for the passage into the unknown. (Parks, 1986, p. 55)

For some of the Reflective Exiles there was a far more gradual and less traumatic move to counter-dependency than that expressed by Jane. Nevertheless people in this reflective faith stance were pushing against anything that reminded them of the EPC church or para-church they had left. This counter-dependency often extended beyond the overt expressions of the EPC community to Christian people as well. As Lucy said:

> *Lucy* I've had a deliberate policy of de-churching myself where I consider I've been indoctrinated for so many years. I really haven't touched Christian books or tapes. I can't stand anything like that. I really don't want to be touched by anyone else's view of God and what my relationship with God should be. You know, so many years of reading that and listening to that . . . I also have a physical aversion to them, or a spiritual or a psychological aversion to anything Christian. In fact, I don't even like being with Christians. I find a lot of their talk is just such trash. I know I'm being very

harsh here, but I'm trying to express how strongly I feel about a lot of Christianity.

When Jane said she no longer read the Bible she stated something which I was to hear again and again from Reflective Exiles. In this counter-dependent phase people push against the previous authority and basis of faith they have held to for so long. For Reflective Exiles this includes 'pushing against' the old ideas of reading the Bible and regular times of prayer. Some would read the Bible occasionally, and most would pray by means of a spontaneous internalized thought process, but not in the ways they experienced in the EPC church. Regarding prayer, Jane said:

Jane I quite often pray spontaneously, automatically, without realizing that I'm doing it. And it's not logical or anything, it's just out of habit. But I don't sort of say my prayers every morning or night.

Deconstruction of faith

Disillusioned Followers	Reflective Exiles
Dependent relationship	Counter-dependent relationship
Received faith	**Deconstruction of faith**

Jenny It has taken a really long time for me to sift out what was the church stuff and what was my faith, and I'm only left with a really little bit, which is a bit disconcerting. I think part of that is because I have no knowledge of any other church or religion – eastern stuff – because it was a really Pentecostal fundamentalist sort of church. I just thought that was the way they all were. So as I found out that that wasn't the case I became really angry and found it difficult to separate out anything that I actually gained for myself and stuff that was just imposed on me. Over the last year I probably have, and I have been left with a small amount of faith and beliefs that I had. And they are not easy to define at all. I think that is because the Pentecostal churches are so hot on rigid definitions and guidelines and black and white things that I think I'm still sort of reacting to that. So I have a really vague definition to things now, and I still think it is maybe a kick back against that. You know, maybe in a year's time I will feel slightly differently.

Interviewer For you does it have a Christian flavour?

Jenny [*long pause*] I guess; yeah; probably – as opposed to what?

Interviewer As opposed to atheistic, or eastern or a Buddhist.

Jenny Yeah, probably if it had a flavour it would be a Christian flavour, but no more than a flavour.

When I asked Jane about which theological questions she was struggling with she replied, 'All of it, basically'. Jenny and Jane are typical of the Reflective Exiles as they are in a process of deconstructing the faith they had received from their time within an EPC church. There appears to be a predictable sequence of the Reflective Exile's questioning, which moves from more peripheral issues towards the very core elements of an EPC faith. Those engaged in this process are deconstructing the faith they had received, accepted and acted within for so many years. To do so is personally a very destabilizing process for them, as their faith has been an important part of their world view, the foundation of important life decisions and an integral part of their sense of identity.

The Reflective Exile's questions are also destabilizing, even threatening, for those around them and especially for those in positions of leadership who feel that it is their responsibility to keep the church growing and vibrant.

Ongoing reflection of faith

Disillusioned Followers	Reflective Exiles
Dependent relationship	Counter-dependent relationship
Received faith	Deconstruction of faith
Unexamined faith	**Ongoing reflection**

The deconstruction of their previously received faith leads people engaged in this process to successively examine the individual components of their faith. People engaged in the deconstruction of their faith remove each article of the belief and value system of their received faith and submit it to a process of ongoing reflection. This process involves a questioning and scrutinizing of the particular belief or value. The important aspect of this process is that each component of their faith is critiqued on the basis of whether the individual will appropriate it as part of their own personal belief or value system. Some faith components are not appropriated, but rejected in part or entirely while others are placed in the 'I don't know' basket and left for a period as 'unknowns'. For many this involves a great deal of thought, discussion and philosophical and theological reflection. For others it is more clearly focused on taking control of their own faith decisions without subjecting their beliefs to a rigorous intellectual critique. For this second group the plausibility of the belief is determined by how it fits with their own experience and life. These people are moving beyond the sense of powerlessness they felt in the EPC church and are now looking at their faith for themselves.

The use in the title of the word 'ongoing' is significant because at this point people are in the midst of the reflective process. This is a process of examination undertaken by the individual, where the arbiter of the process, deciding what is accepted or rejected, is the person themself. In this 'ongoing reflection' individuals must assume responsibility, and take ultimate authority for the questioning, critiquing and resolution of their examination. The process of ongoing reflection, evident in the Reflective Exiles' interview scripts, moves successively from peripheral issues to increasingly more foundational faith beliefs and values.

The ironic twist in the process of deconstruction and examination being undertaken by the Reflective Exiles is that while still members of EPC churches, many of them were told that if they had doubts they should examine their hearts. Obviously what is implied here is that if they had doubts the problem was theirs and they had to sort themselves out. Ironically, the doubts and questions of the Reflective Exiles have led them to reflect on their faith rather than consider what is wrong within themselves. That is, to reflect critically on the core beliefs, values and expected behaviours of the EPC faith as a result of the anomalies they have found within their previous faith package rather than immediately consider they have failed in some way.

Many of the interviewees in this faith stance mention a new awareness and trust in their own feelings. For some this is a move contrary to what they were taught within the church where it was customary for evangelicals to see feelings as untrustworthy and unreliable and to trust the tenets of the faith rather than their own feelings.

> *Fiona* I was trying to find a structure that was flexible enough and also got to the real issues rather than just 'Here is the Bible study and what do we think about this?' But rather than opinions, we can talk about opinions but you can miss the real issues. Sometimes the real issues are – I am hurt in this area, and I am angry in this area, or I fear. And if it doesn't have an apparent spiritual meaning to it, then it's often sort of written off because it just doesn't fit into our frame of reference for what is religious or spiritual or Christian.

In the process of deconstructing and reflecting on their faith, many of the Reflective Exiles develop a new trust for their emotions and intuitions, which they use as part of the judgement they bring to each segment of the faith they are re-evaluating. Although for most the weighing of their faith involves thoughtfulness and the search for new understanding, many also mentioned a renewed trust in their own emotions and intuitions.

The outcome of this ongoing reflection of their faith leads them to one of three decisions. Either the statement of belief being examined is appropriated personally, or put in the 'don't know' basket, or discarded as something they no longer believe and perhaps wish they never had. Below are the comments of three Reflective Exiles as they examine their faith.

> *Lucy* I'm a lot more hesitant now, because I don't know what's right and wrong any more. When I was in church and doing all the churchy things I felt I knew the answers to everything. There was always an answer and always a way of looking at things. Things were very black and white in those days. Now I feel that I don't know the answers to anything. I know there's a God but that's about all I know.
>
> I don't even know if there's a Jesus Christ. I know he existed but I just don't know about the whole Christian, you know, Jesus thing any more. But I do know and my conversion shows me that, and lots of experiences since, show me without a doubt that there is a God. And that's the God that I have a relationship with. The only sure thing that I have in my faith is God. All the others I'm just not sure about.

Dave I don't know about prayer. I've been through the positive confession, you know, demand your rights and all this sort of thing with God. If you confess it, it is going to be yours. You know Scripture says it. Earlier on I went through all that. And everything I confessed or believed for never came. But I would like to think that there is just a simple communion with God. Ideally I would just love to know the scripture in Genesis where they spoke with God in the cool of the evening. I mean, that is real nice, there is nothing hard about that. And the grace of God, you know, God maybe is willing to have a bit of a chat to us at times.

Ruth The Bible used to be the very word of God, the very direction of my daily being, my daily direction. But now I don't see the Bible as the absolute word of God. It is an ancient book, I see it as a very respectable book, a book of very wise sayings, and really these people did meet Jesus Christ. But to me it was a heavenly book. Now it is an earthly book. I am still grappling with that.

The 'I don't know' does not indicate that the leavers are shrugging off their faith questions and concerns. Nor is it an 'I don't know' that is void of ideas, thoughts and arguments regarding the faith issue at hand. Rather it is a response that recognizes that as of yet they have not resolved a profound dilemma. The leavers are no longer satisfied by simplistic solutions and are conscious, often very conscious, of realities that previous certainties failed to incorporate. It is, as Ward and Wild express it, 'an "I don't know" that is paradoxically full of knowledge'.[4] Hence the faith stance of the Reflective Exiles is seen not as a rejection of their previous faith but a realization of its inadequacy in the light of their wider experience. It is a pursuit of a more satisfying sense of 'truth' that does not seek to merely wallpaper over the cracks of its own incompleteness, which the Reflective Exiles perceive is often being done in the faith claims prominent within the EPC churches.

A hesitant faith

Disillusioned Followers	Reflective Exiles
Dependent relationship	Counter-dependent relationship
Received faith	Deconstruction of faith
Unexamined faith	Ongoing reflection
Bold	**Hesitant**

Heather My current faith beliefs? I am not sure that I have many. I have all this stuff that I have done at Bible College that I think offered a credible faith. I am not quite sure that I sit within it, but it is there if that makes sense. I think I have sort of put it into storage for a while, really. You know, 25 years of going to church every Sunday. Twice a day for a long time. Twenty-five years of praying before you make decisions. Twenty-five years of all these sorts of ways of doing things. It is not just whether you have corn-flakes for breakfast sort of thing. It becomes part of your core – who you are as a person. And when that suddenly goes with sort of question marks – it is not something that you take off like a coat. So I have put it in a drawer, and it is there, and maybe I will open it again sometime, but not at the moment.

Heather, like Jane, has put her faith questions into cold storage for a while. Jane said, 'I don't know where I am as far as believing in God, or who Jesus was and things like that. I'm not sure about that now, but I don't sort of feel I have to know.' For leavers like Jane and Heather part of the exiting process is a putting down of the faith issues. People in this 'reflective stage' of faith do not have high degrees of internal motivation to pursue the answers to their faith questions. This lack of enthusiasm and energy for their faith is not surprising considering the lack of certainty and confidence a deconstructing and counter-dependent faith affords them.

The reflective phase appears to be a difficult phase within which to navigate a positive faith journey on your own. Ironically, at the very time people are feeling they want to push away from the church community their doing so is likely to alienate them from one source of external support resources that might help them navigate beyond their present faith position.

In the next chapter we will meet those who are moving beyond the Reflective Exile phase towards rebuilding an autonomous and integrated faith. This is the journey of some of the Reflective Exiles, but not all. The Reflective Exiles phase becomes for many a static place – a permanent place of exile. Those who do move on towards an autonomous and integrated faith are joined in the next chapter by those who leave their church when they have substantially navigated the reflective phase while still participating, however loosely, within their church community.

NOTES

1 The word 'meta' also draws our attention to two key ingredients of 'meta-grumbles'. First, 'meta' is part of the progression from micro to macro to meta. This therefore implies that 'meta-grumbles' form the largest and most fundamental of grumbles to do with someone's faith. And second, the prefix 'meta' means 'change' as in metabolism, metamorphosis, metaphysical and in the Greek word *metanoia* (to change one's mind or 'repent'). Therefore the term 'meta-grumbles' implies a fundamental change in the basis of one's faith. The term 'meta-grumbles' is drawn from Cohen and Taylor (1992, p. 14), who describe meta-grumbles as attempts to escape Lyotard's concept of meta-narratives ('which lay claim to an over-arching understanding of human nature, social progress and cultural change' [op.cit., p. 12]). Meta-grumbles indicate a dissatisfaction with such meta-narratives as form the 'paramount reality' in which we all live.

2 The 'counter-dependent' concept is drawn from Parks' work (1986, p. 55).

3 For some interviewees this counter-dependence began while they were still involved in the church. In such situations, while there may not have been a physical distancing and rejection of faith contents there had nevertheless been a self-conscious distancing at least within their own minds.

4 Ward and Wild (1995, pp. 121–2), speaking of their involvement with women leaving Christian churches, state: 'In the context of the struggle for meaning, for community and for integrity, two things keep recurring in conversations with other women and in our lives. They are the values of "silence" and of "not knowing" . . . Silence is the language of "non-knowing". It is also the ground in which both love and knowledge can grow and flourish.'

SIX

Transitional explorers

The crucial turning point for Mark came after he had been leading a church group supporting ex-psychiatric patients who were moving out of residential care into the community. For Mark this meant time dealing with severely depressed people, and people who were reacting badly to medication or who had withdrawn themselves from regular medication. Many of these people had been institutionalized for long periods and were now struggling to make their way in the wider society. At times Mark was involved in working with people who were threatening to take their own lives or were suffering from delusions of grandeur or evil. A formative part of this work was a friendship he built with a paranoid schizophrenic. Dealing with his friend and others in the group raised a lot of questions for Mark about his faith. 'Does God heal schizophrenia? You know, all those really good ones', he says with a quizzical smile on his face. For Mark this was not some academic or distant question, but one of a cluster of pressing personal issues confronting his faith.

Since becoming a Christian at the age of 20, Mark had been very actively involved in two churches. The first was a large Pentecostal church where he participated for nearly four years. Speaking of his involvement in this church he describes it, saying, 'At that time it was pretty much full on commitment. You know you smoked it, breathed it, twice on Sundays. I was involved in the youth group, leading or running the youth group, going to a home group, all that sort of stuff – right into it.' Later, because of leadership struggles in the church and a growing number of friends at another church, he made the move to a large charismatic Baptist church. It was through this church that he became involved in the psychiatric group. But again this was only part of his involvement. Mark was an active member of one of the home groups, a number of church outreaches and a member of the church evangelism programme.

Mark I was involved in trying to do evangelism in our area . . . sort of a door-to-door thing. So we went around with these surveys; when I think of it now it was just a foot in the door. We were doing a survey, but really we wanted to talk about God.

Perhaps because of the faith questions being raised by his leadership of the psychiatric group more than any other single reason, Mark enrolled to spend three years at a theological college studying towards a bachelor's degree in theology. For Mark this was a stimulating faith environment.

Mark Parts of it I thoroughly, absolutely enjoyed. I loved the contradiction. We did biblical formal, source criticism, redaction criticism[1] and all that stuff. And people were just about throwing their faith away, and I was just lapping it up. This stuff made sense, the whole idea of the different sources and having a different perspective, not being synthesized and all the 'jots and tittles' weren't exactly the same. Rather they were all from different points of view. Yeah, I liked the fact that all kinds of things were being knocked over and re-formed. Preconceptions, all of these amazing delicious new ideas. You know, I love new ideas. So that part of it I really thoroughly enjoyed.

When Mark returned to his home church complete with his Bachelor of Theology he was struck by the question of what he should do now. The church seemed to have high expectations of him and so did he, but these were being radically undermined by a period of personal confusion and despair. As he says, 'As best as I can fathom, basically I think I got depressed . . . all the classic depression signs, waking up early in the morning, not sleeping, not enjoying anything . . .' Throughout this period he felt he was not meeting either his own or the church's expectations of him.

Mark You build an amazing amount of self-expectation after doing three years at theological college. And even before that, the whole Christian emphasis is on doing and being; doing things for God and being a particular kind of person. When you don't meet up to your own expectations of what a Christian should do and be, a crisis takes place. Suddenly you almost feel powerless to do and be what you should do and be, and you go to church. I went and I would hear all these messages about what I should do and be. And the word 'should' is probably something that still rings in my ears now. Something that characterizes church is the word 'should'.

This led to feelings of guilt and a sense of failure. At times Mark said he felt quite selfish and self-centred and was only dragging himself around. He tried to explain where he was at to one of the leaders of the church:

> *Mark* I remember trying to tell a guy at church once how I was feeling. He just said nothing. He couldn't deal with it. He was a guy who you would say was a mature person, but he just couldn't deal with it. Another day he asked me if he could pray with me and I told him no (ha ha). I thought, you can't even listen to me, you haven't even earned the right. Maybe the word 'earned' is a bit harsh, but that was how I felt.

Over a period of months Mark drifted out of this church and had a period of six months completely outside any church participation before tentatively joining a mainstream liturgical church. He says that he now goes occasionally, sits at the back but is otherwise uninvolved. During his six-month break from church he took a mild course of anti-depressants, went to counselling and joined a group of questioners like himself who had been brought together by a Christian psychotherapist.

For Mark, the group, the decision to have a period of time outside the church and the insights he gained through his theological training together helped him to move through the reflective faith stage to where he is now at, a Transitional Explorer.

Mark represents a further group of leavers, which I have called Transitional Explorers. These leavers displayed an emerging sense of ownership of their faith. This was shown in a confidence of faith, a clear decision to move from a deconstruction of their received faith to a re-appropriation of some elements of Christian faith and giving energy to building a new self-owned faith. To varying degrees, this faith incorporates elements of the previous church-based faith. What has changed is that these elements have now been tested and found to be valid and worthy of being retained to the level of satisfaction necessary for the individual involved. To use an analogy from the courtroom, the internal jury has reached a verdict on these faith elements and now sees them as being plausible 'beyond reasonable doubt'. What constitutes 'reasonable doubt' varies from person to person. As mentioned earlier, for some the examination process involves rigorous theological and philosophical debate through reading and/or interaction with others. For others, 'reasonable doubt' is based more on personal experience and what is plausible to them at an intuitive, almost 'gut-feeling' level.

The Transitional Explorers represented 18 per cent of those interviewed. Many of these people had left their EPC church while their faith position could best be described as reflective, and had since moved on into a transitional faith phase. Others had left the church during this transitional faith period.

As shown in Figure 6.1, the transitional phase is seen as a progression out of the reflective phase. Although some people move through this reflective phase while still participating in a church they nevertheless go through a reflective phase before the beginning of the transitional phase. Those who stayed connected to their church during the reflective phase spoke of moving to a more marginal involvement and a more detached perspective.

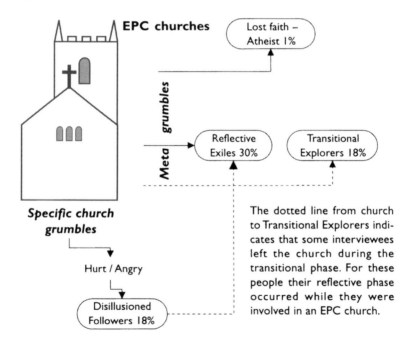

Figure 6.1 Journeys of faith outside of the EPC church
Trajectory 3 – Transitional Explorers

This group are called explorers because of the ways they are finding and rebuilding a faith for themselves. Transitional Explorers are those whose focus is on scouting out or opening up a new faith journey. The focus of such leavers is not on what they have left, as it is for the Reflective Exiles, but on beginning to find a new way forward. As Roger Grainger writes:

> For the new situation to live the old one must die. Thus there is always a crucial point 'between', a point representing the condition after the old state of affairs has come to an end and before the new one has actually begun. This is the moment of real change, the pivotal moment that has no movement of itself, but permits movement to take place. (Grainger, 1993, p. 48)

The transitional phase represents the time beyond this pivotal moment. It is distinct from the exile phase because the individual is now beginning to find a way forward. It is the move depicted in Joshua which records the crucial transition the nation of Israel took in the journey from exile in the wilderness to the promised land.

> On the tenth day of the first month the people went up from the Jordan and camped at Gilgal on the eastern border of Jericho. And Joshua set up at Gilgal the twelve stones they had taken out of the Jordan. He said to the Israelites, 'In the future when your descendants ask their fathers, "What do these stones mean?" tell them, "Israel crossed the Jordan on dry ground." ' (Joshua 4.19–22)

The crossing of the Jordan represented the crucial transitional point in the journey. Their journey had not ended with the crossing of the Jordan but it had entered a new phase. A crucial border had been crossed. The placing of the stones acted as a reminder that this transition had occurred. The people described here as Transitional Explorers have also crossed some crucial boundaries and this new category reflects this. This is a move from critical distance to a new engagement with faith. During this exploratory phase the individual is finding and pioneering a new faith direction for themselves, a faith direction which, as we shall later see, may have a number of similarities with the EPC faith they have previously left.

Inner-dependency

Disillusioned Followers	Reflective Exiles	Transitional Explorers
Dependent relationship	Counter-dependency	**Inner-dependency**

Where the faith of the Reflective Exiles was characterized by a counter-dependence on the EPC community, its beliefs, expectations and values, the faith of the Transitional Explorers is characterized by a developing sense of inner-dependence[2] for the validity and nurture of one's own faith. Mark talks about the group he joined as being 'really, really good' because it focused more on what was going on inside.

> *Mark* Probably one important thing that happened to me was I got involved in a group . . . which has a focus less on thinking and more on feeling. It was much more feeling-oriented, so they tended to ask not why, but what do you think; not why do you feel the way you do, but what do you feel? So it was really good, really helpful, and that was to one degree or another the saving of my faith. These people, who I did consider to be solid Christians, were actually able to cope with my questioning, didn't shut down on me and didn't get sort of squeamish. They were able to cope, with my swearing or whatever. That was very reassuring.

Mark saw this as being quite different to the approach he experienced within the church. His perception of the church was that it was focused on being proactive and on what people *should* be doing as Christians.

> *Mark* I think if I could say what the church could have done more of, it would have been to focus less on what you should be and more on what you are. And just the whole accepting of what you are. Not the superficial 'God accepts you for what you are', but go into it in some depth. Sort of mull on it a bit and soak it in. Maybe some people would call it a bit depressing, but I think there would be a surprising number of people out there who would actually find it really good.

This is a shift from a dependency, or a counter-dependency on the church environment to a new, quite different base – one of inner-dependency. Here the crucial issues are inner, self-oriented issues relating to one's emotions, intuitions and feelings. As Parks says, 'Here a person begins to listen within, with a new respect and trust for the truth of his or her 'own insides'. That is, the person begins to listen and be responsible to the self as a source of authority and as an object of care' (Parks, 1986, p. 58). With this can come a shifting understanding, perhaps especially for women, of their role as caregivers. Where previously they have extended care to others even at the expense of themselves there can now often be an increased awareness of the need for self-care.[3]

At this point Mark was quite clear that he was completely at a loss as to where he fitted in the traditional church structure, but within the group he had found a place where his questions, concerns and feelings were accepted. As he put it, 'Here was a place where I did fit – very much. Here my questions were not just tolerated, but also enjoyed. The process was more than accepted, it was enjoyed.' The people who went along to the group with Mark had similar questions and a similar concern to find a relevant inner faith that dealt adequately with the deeper concerns of their 'inner selves'.

> *Mark* The whole emphasis on self-giving has changed too. I recognize that it is a desirable state to be able to give. It can be a desirable state, as long as you are not co-dependent and all those complicated things. That self-giving to me has another side to it that was never emphasized in church or wasn't thrashed around quite enough. I think people, if I just speak from experience here, have to have a self to give in the first place. If you haven't got a strong self, give whatever little you have. People would argue about this, I'm sure, but my view, to deny what little self you have can at sometimes be almost impossible.

The sense of inner-dependency is very clear in the beliefs and actions of transitional people as well. Mark says:

> *Mark* I suppose at the one end God does everything, at the other we are the author of our own destiny. I probably am pretty much at the own destiny end now, while acknowledging that theology and all kinds of other things conspire to say that he does act. So I hold that quite loosely, and would like to talk about it more with various people. I don't quite understand what I do believe. I know that I believe God is up there supervising events in a global sense. I think he gives us a lot of responsibility for our own lives that we wouldn't wish to bear, but I think that is the fact of it. Many of the

decisions that we make are our own as adult Christians and I think what I tend to believe in is some kind of a spirit-illuminated wisdom. But it is a wisdom where God is very much a gentleman in the process. He very much allows us to trip and make stupid mistakes.

Like Mark, people in the transitional phase are developing a solidifying inner foundation and validity for their faith. For Parks this inner-dependency does not equate with independence because 'other sources of authority may still hold credible power, but now one can recognize and value also the authority of the self' (Parks, 1986, p. 57).

A reconstruction of faith

Disillusioned Followers	Reflective Exiles	Transitional Explorers
Dependent relationship	Counter-dependency	Inner-dependency
Received faith	Deconstruction of faith	**Reconstruction of faith**

Mark, and a number of the other members of the group he attends, are beginning to reconstruct a personal faith. The process of deconstructing faith has ceased, at least for now, and they have begun to personally accept the validity of some elements of their previous faith. These personally appropriated faith elements can then be fitted together as a new faith construction process begins. For most of the members of this transitional group some of these faith elements have strong similarities with those they had received from the EPC church.

> *Maree* I still tithe regularly. I have carried that on over the years, but not to a church. I decided early on that I wasn't going to tithe to buildings. So a lot goes through child sponsorship. It is 10 per cent and that is a principle that I won't ever give up. I believe that God gives to us and that whole thing of the gift of life is really precious.

Almost inevitably some of the values, expectations and beliefs of the EPC church community are also rejected while other beliefs, expectations and values are incorporated in the reconstruction of this more personally appropriated faith. For many of these transitional people there is a replacement of some of the more confining EPC faith statements with wider Christian interpretations. For example, here interviewees generally expressed a wider understanding of salvation than would typically be part of the EPC faith they had previously received. Many would now also hold to quite different interpretations of heaven and hell and afterlife states. Coupled with this is a wider acceptance of practices that would normally be frowned upon in the EPC community. For example, a preparedness to accept active homosexuality as an acceptable lifestyle, or unmarried, but stable, heterosexual partnerships.

While for many the reconstruction of faith involves many aspects of their previous beliefs, values and expectations, it may also include a number of new elements. These new elements are wider in what is seen as being acceptable to those held to within the EPC community these people have left. Where the Reflective Exiles were engaged in a process of deconstruction and subsequent examination of the components of their received faith, the Transitional Explorers have now examined a number of their faith components and found them useful for the new self-constructed faith that they are building. Many Transitional Explorers are also incorporating other beliefs, values and ways of behaving that are not components of the EPC faith package.

One reason transitional faith people find that they still don't fit in an EPC church community is their incorporation of these new faith components that lie outside a typical EPC faith package. It would seem reasonable to suppose that those who have incorporated a large number of different faith components experience the greatest sense of discomfort with EPC churches.

Dianne I have a very, very dear homosexual friend, a man who has got incredible love for other people. They [the church] treated him like shit. But he went on loving. I really believe there are concepts of homosexual love. I didn't see that as something as dirty or degrading, like the way the church put it. I'm not saying whether I personally believe it or not. For me it's not what I want for my life, but I don't actually think that Jesus actually cares too much. He was more interested in those bloody hypocritical Pharisees who went round preaching this and doing that and doing something else.

An emerging self-ownership of faith

Disillusioned Followers	Reflective Exiles	Transitional Explorers
Dependent relationship	Counter-dependency	Inner-dependency
Received faith	Deconstruction of faith	Reconstruction of faith
Unexamined faith	Ongoing reflection	**Emerging self-ownership**

Linked with the reconstruction of faith and the self-appropriation of a growing number of faith elements is the sense of an emerging self-ownership of faith. Where the Reflective Exiles are confused and hesitant about their faith, the Transitional Explorers have an emerging sense of what their faith entails, and a new acceptance of this as their own faith system.

> *Stephen* I've always believed in God. I had a very powerful conversion. I have no doubt about it whatsoever. Nothing could basically rock me from that faith. My concept of God perhaps has changed. With my marriage breaking up, I've spent that many days on my hands and knees on the floor sobbing my heart out, just crying out to God. Week after week and nothing happened, nothing and I ask why. But I've stopped all that now and stopped the questioning and just accept it. 'Well, it's in your hands, it's out of my hands and that is OK.' It hasn't changed my faith in God and who he is. But I haven't gone on in church. I just find I can't do that. I find I'm in this transition period, I believe. I believe I will go back in time and I'll go back there with different eyes, and not as naive as what I was before.

A strengthening faith

Disillusioned Followers	Reflective Exiles	Transitional Explorers
Dependent relationship	Counter-dependency	Inner-dependency
Received faith	Deconstruction of faith	Reconstruction of faith
Unexamined faith	Ongoing reflection	Emerging self-ownership
Bold	Hesitant	**Strengthening**

During the transitional phase people are prepared to give more energy and time to their faith. This contrasts with the putting down of faith often characteristic of the reflective phase. The transitioners are engaging with their faith through attendance at courses, fringe involvement in church services, their own reading and study or through a group that has a Christian focus. As well as this re-engagement with their faith, many of the transitional people mentioned a hope of being more involved in the church in future. Mark, for example, expressed a desire to be actively involved in the church, but as an independent person who would be appreciated for who he was, and was able to challenge others when they were accepting things in a way that he felt was inappropriate.

Transition to an alternative faith

For another 6 per cent of those interviewed a large proportion of their reconstructed faith drew on elements outside of Christian faith. Two of these people would now call themselves New Agers rather than Christians, while the other five as a result of the deconstruction process, have rejected some, if not all, of the EPC faith elements. They continue to reject their previous faith to the point that they have accepted an agnostic faith stance. In order to identify this alternative faith journey I have categorized these people as 'Transitioning to an Alternative Faith'.

Susan had been a staff member of a Christian mission organization for five years before returning to her previous career and her rural hometown. Initially she was very involved in the local church and the youth group and outreaches to young people in the area, but as her own questions came to the surface her involvement in these areas dropped off. Struggling with her own childhood history of sexual abuse, a vague feeling that maybe she was gay and a church that was completely unsympathetic to the desperate questions she had, she moved out of the church and began to take on more of the New Age-based beliefs of some of her workmates. In the process of moving out of the church and for the last few years that she has been outside the church, she has put aside many of her received beliefs. When I interviewed her, she said that she saw herself more as a 'spiritual person than a Christian'. Although she continues with some of her Christian belief system she has stripped this down to a small refined core and added a number of other beliefs, values and practices.

Susan I don't see Jesus so much as the Son of God, but I see him more as someone who came to earth to teach us lessons and show us the right way to live. And that he was a really special person, and he was one who cared about women and treated women as equals. And I respect him for that. But I think there have been other prophets that have come as well. I still retain him as part of my faith.

I don't read the Bible any more. I've got one – I haven't thrown it out. I've got it sitting on my bookcase. I just see it as collection of stories, except for my favourite Psalm 91. I do read that from time to time. But I don't actually read the Bible like I used to. I don't sit down and actually sit there and pray as such: I talk to, well, more to Jesus, I just say things during the day and communicate. I don't sit down and have a set prayer time any more, like I used to.

Susan has rejected the rest of the EPC faith package, including God, about whom she claims she had become a bit 'anti'.[4] Now she describes God as 'good orderly direction'. 'I would rather see God as a good energy force.' To this residue of Christian faith she has added beliefs in rebirthing, trauma guides, reincarnation and an array of goddesses. She describes her new faith system as 'so anti-Christian when I come to think about some of the things I believe'.

> *Susan* I think what happened was that was the time when I was really searching. I got involved with Elizabeth Kübler-Ross grief work, I did her life–death transition workshop and Kübler-Ross is really into reincarnation. I started to get into rebirthing and I had a couple of past-life experiences, I mean, because of my Christian faith I could not comprehend reincarnation or coming back. So when I did these two rebirths and had past-life experiences, I thought, 'What is happening to me?' They were so clear and I could describe everything and the feelings that went with it and I died. I actually died in these two. And in one of them I drowned, because I was on the *Titanic*. I had never read about the *Titanic*, so I went and got this book and went through it and everything I said was really accurate. In the death thing I actually went up to God – this bright light again, that light that I had before – and saw my angel there. I have always known that I had a guardian angel and I've always seen her right from when I was little, because that helped me get through a lot of my trauma stuff. And the angel was there and this presence that I knew was God.

Some other transitional people have systematically rejected each aspect of the EPC faith in the process of deconstructing their faith to the point that they would choose to call themselves agnostics rather than Christians or adherents to any other faith. For them their faith has been replaced with more humanist and pragmatic beliefs. Bruce, an ex-minister who trained in a theological college for three years and then led a very prosperous charismatic church for seven years, says:

> *Bruce* I now think the whole link between prayer and positive self-affirmation, self-belief and positive belief in things happening is very, very close. And when I look back on what I used to define as spiritual prayer to God I now find the same thing happening in totally different areas; when people are simply self-affirming, and some are visualizing and seeing things happen. Equally strong results. So I now think that maybe they're both describing the same thing and probably that's where I'm at.
>
> One of the things I've worked through over the last few months is in my job. When I was minister I used to stand and speak to people and believe that this was God's word and it was important they heard it, and there was sort of a driving energy. Now I train people in business areas. If I'm actually convinced that it's critical they get this thing sorted out to change, there's a whole energy in there that's not in it if I'm just going to go through the routine. I kind of think, 'Now hang on, where's the difference?' I suspect it's the same thing again, but with a different label.

Bruce's wife Alison says they gave away praying and reading the Bible and nothing happened – life went on as it always had. She says, 'I just think that faith and prayer and that sort of thing is valuable but not because . . . I mean for some people it's valuable, but not because there is an external being answering it, but because of the sort of positive energy that is created or something.' It got to the point where when she looked at her faith she thought, 'Well, what was that?' When I met Bruce and Alison they had left their church. For Bruce this meant not only leaving his church but his career as a minister. For a while they had moved to an evangelical church but they became uncomfortable there, so they moved to a more theologically liberal church. Today they are right outside the church with no intention of returning. As Alison said, 'We have tried them all.' Bruce and Alison hope that their children don't get caught up in some fundamentalist Christianity, and actively protect them from church involvement. They do however allow them to attend the odd Christian camp, explaining that one week a year will not be a great influence. The people who make up this group of agnostics are most closely linked to the long-term reflective faith people who, in the process of deconstructing their faith, have placed each faith segment into the 'I don't know' or rejected piles.

It appears that there are two significant factors that allow this relatively small group of people to reject the final core elements of their previous faith. The first of these is an absence of a clear personal experience of 'God at work in their lives' to which they can finally refer. It is the presence of such an experience that provides the final foundational legitimation of faith for many of the Reflective Exiles who would claim they have not left their faith.

The second factor appears to be a degree of personal courage which allows these people to jettison the final residue of previous Christian beliefs. That this requires courage is not at all surprising considering the teachings prevalent in the EPC church regarding the fate of those who reject their faith in God. Such rejection is generally considered tantamount to a 'guaranteed one-way trip to hell'. After years of accepting

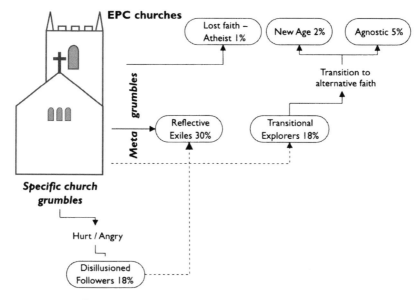

Figure 6.2 Journeys of faith outside of the EPC church
Trajectory 4 – Transitioning to an Alternative Faith

this kind of teaching and internalization of such extreme ramifications for such a rejection of God, it can hardly be surprising to hear that some people hang on to a faith confession long after such a confession has passed any personal use-by date.

In order to acknowledge the transitional move of this group of people towards an alternative faith system we need to incorporate them into the diagrammatic illustration of church leavers. This is shown in Figure 6.2. These alternative faith Transitional Explorers have begun journeying on a faith path that has beliefs, values and expected behaviours that clearly diverge from the EPC version of Christian faith or any other stream of the Christian faith.

Conclusion

The Transitional Explorers are characterized as having crossed a crucial transition point between doubt and an emerging sense of trust in their faith, between suspicion and openness, between faith deconstruction and faith reconstruction and between an ongoing reflectiveness and a new self-ownership of their faith. It is a transition that is hard to clearly identify as it involves a new inner-dependency that motivates and sustains the journey of faith. Although difficult to quantify it is nevertheless a significant transition, one that marks the beginnings of a fundamental transformation in a person's faith. For the majority of people identified as Transitional Explorers this involved a transformation within their Christian faith. However, for a minority this transition led to the move to a new faith basis. For two of those interviewed a New Age faith was appropriated and five others moved to an agnostic faith stance. In the next chapter we will meet the final grouping of EPC church leavers, the Integrated Wayfinders, who represent those who have, in faith terms, moved beyond this transitional stage to a more fully integrated Christian faith.

NOTES

1 Redaction criticism is one form of exegetical critique used by theologians in the process of understanding the Scriptures.
2 The term 'inner-dependence' is taken from Parks' (1986) development of faith.

3 Parks continues, stating: 'Carol Gilligan's study (1982) suggests a corresponding motion in the dimension of care. People (especially women) who have previously tended to extend care almost exclusively to others to the neglect of the self (because only others had the authority to claim care) can now extend care also to the self (who now has the authority to claim care)' (Parks, 1986, pp.57–8).

4 This is related to the idea of God as Father which she found she no longer related to. 'I could no longer cope with him as father.' Much of this was related to her experience of her own father in childhood.

SEVEN

Integrated wayfinders

It was after being narrowly defeated as a candidate for Parliament that Rob began to rethink the basis of the EPC faith he had championed for 14 years.

Rob I almost ended up in Parliament as a Christian MP with a perceived mandate to promote the Christian perspective . . . I knew that the things I was standing for were clearly based on the 'Word of God', but during my canvassing I began to perceive that our stance was lacking in compassion. I had been knocking on hundreds of doors and people kept asking questions like 'Are you going to stop schools teaching evolution, and are you going to stamp out sex education, are you going to hang all the poofters?' We were looked at as neo-Nazis. I found that there were many, many good people out there who were just as concerned about social trends as I was, and they had very reasonable but non-biblical views of how to deal with the issues. As I tried to reason with them the bases of their views made an awful lot of sense to me.

I realized that my counsel always ultimately went back to the Word of God. I'd say, 'Well, the Word of God says this, and that makes it right.' But the more I argued the more I began to realize, rather uncomfortably, that while I was consistent with Scripture, the arguments we had derived from it were shallow and simplistic, and often out of step with reality. I also saw that what we would have produced, if we'd had the opportunity to bring about a 'Christianized' society, was going to be rather dour and loveless, puritanical, like an Islamic fundamentalist state, full of passion for imposing the Laws of God, but indifferent to those who lived under them. What these people who had thrown out the Bible generations ago said was also internally consistent, and it actually made just as much sense, if not more, and was often more compassionate.

I felt in myself that what I was promoting was all wrong. It was scriptural, but it was wrong. When the election was over I felt very uncomfortable with my faith, with my church, and even with my friends.

It caused me to really question the whole Christian perspective. Which was the right view?

These questions led to other questions, including the whole creation–evolution debate. As an analytical chemist, Rob read widely on the issue and concluded that the creationist arguments just didn't stand up. The end result was a sense of being required to support ideas that he couldn't accept as being truthful. Serious examination of this tenet of his faith led him to look into other areas. He looked at Christian spirituality and mysticism, psychology and philosophy, which led on to readings about Hinduism, Islam, Taoism and Buddhism. Through these studies and his own reflection Rob began seriously to question the dogmatic confidence and exclusivism of evangelical Christians and their interpretation of the Bible. In his reflective phase he examined how the Bible came together, and came to the view that the way evangelicals used it was not the way it was intended to be used. The end result for Rob was a complete re-evaluation of his faith.

> *Rob* I was having to rethink all of the stuff that I'd believed, right down to bedrock, and ask myself, Well, what do I really believe now?

It is therefore clear that Rob has travelled a similar faith questioning and re-examining journey as that discussed in the last two chapters. The point, however, is that Rob has come to a different place in his faith than that expressed by the Reflective Exiles or the Transitional Explorers. Rob describes the process using a building analogy.

> *Rob* We look at the Holy Spirit's ministry to us and he is like pouring in the concrete, the rules that could be expressed as the ethics of the New Testament or the rules of the Old Testament are simply the boxing. You know, you pour concrete into boxing, the boxing is there to provide shape and restrain. And he pours it in and it sets, and you take the boxing away, you throw them down, meaningless, they are simply there to do a brief job. What is important is what's in the boxing. I feel that so much of our whole church ethos is constantly into boxing, not letting the concrete set, not even getting the concrete in there in a lot of the cases, but the whole purpose of your church experience is to provide the boxing into which the Holy Spirit can run and become your personality.

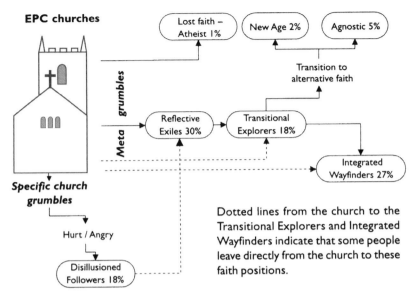

Figure 7.1 Journeys of faith outside of the EPC church
Trajectory 5 – Integrated Wayfinders

As Rob speaks of his faith, he leans forward in his chair and a spark of enthusiasm comes into his eyes. He exhibits a high degree of conviction towards his faith, saying:

> *Rob* I think my faith now is far more personally profound than it's ever been. I have felt total confidence that I am closer to God now than I have ever been, even though I've pulled away from all the things I'm supposed to do. I'm reading the Bible and I feel comfortable in the Bible. I'm praying. I'm feeling more comfortable praying. I'm trying to develop the attitude of prayer, the practising the presence of God type of prayer . . . I know that my value for God is not what I can do for him but all the value is what he can do for me. So I know that what I am becoming is important to him, not the outward things . . . What I understand now is that life is about becoming the kind of person that you could become and you have this degree of freedom to explore and delight God, almost surprise God, with what can be done with a life. I see this as being the aim of it. I don't see Christian service as being the aim of life; it's a by-product of spirituality.

93

It is this conviction of faith that is now more clearly articulated which distinguishes this grouping of leavers from the Transitional Explorers. I have categorized people with faith stances such as Rob's as Integrated Wayfinders. As we shall see shortly, in terms of their energy for and sense of commitment to their faith, the Integrated Wayfinders are closer to the Disillusioned Followers than to either of the other groupings of leavers. There are, however, two key differences that separate them. First, when pushed, the Disillusioned Followers will eventually account for their faith by reference to either an unexamined confidence in the Bible, personal experience of the supernatural or an external source of authority. In contrast, the Integrated Wayfinders may well ground their beliefs on the Bible or personal experience but it is a reliance on experience or Scripture that has been critically examined and found to be plausible. The Integrated Wayfinders will tell you about the questioning and evaluation processes that they employed as well as the strong convictional basis for their faith.

The second means of distinguishing the two groups is the degree of identification with and acceptance of other faith beliefs and philosophies as also embracing truth. The Disillusioned Followers remain comparatively narrow and rigid in their beliefs and values, whereas the Integrated Wayfinders have incorporated statements of truth, beliefs and values from wider faith backgrounds than the EPC church. This impression is reinforced by the openness expressed by Integrated Wayfinders towards people of other belief systems. These people are more accepting, less defensive and more willing to enter into open discussion.

The word integrated is defined as 'complete, combined into a whole'. The faith expressed by people at this phase exhibits a completeness not found in the previous faith phases. Where the Transitional Explorers are in the process of reconstructing their faith and developing an emerging self-ownership, the integrated faith people have to all intents and purposes completed this faith reconstruction work. While there is a sense in which the integrated faith is also still open and being constantly redefined and adapted, the major faith examination is now complete.

The process could be likened to the building of a house out of timber from a previous home. The first part of the process involves moving out of the old home and carefully tearing it down. In the demolition phase the timber, window and door frames, roofing materials and fittings are assessed for their usefulness as materials for the new house. This process is what I have called the reflective phase. The next part of the process involves building the new house out of the materials retrieved from the old one and the incorporation of new materials. This is the transitional phase, where much of the structural faith building is done. Finally, the house is complete and liveable and the person is able to move in. This final phase may include minor ongoing work to the house, rooms may still need to be painted, repairs made and at times modifications of various sizes undertaken. Although this work is ongoing, the basic structure of the home is complete and it now affords a safe place for the individual to live. This final phase in the faith journey is what I have called the integrated faith phase, because here the structure of the faith is complete and the person is able to appropriate it as their own faith system. People at this final phase, like the builder of the home, may well be involved in ongoing questioning and occasional periods of faith re-evaluation (on some occasions involving quite substantial re-evaluations), but the major structural work is now done.

The term 'integrated' is also descriptive of a second aspect of these people's faith, in that they are seeking to integrate their faith into all aspects of their lives. These people, like no other grouping previously discussed, have a more fully orbed faith that seeks to integrate the physical, mental, emotional, sexual, relational and spiritual aspects of themselves in a way deeply connected with their faith. Hence people at this faith phase are very aware of the deeper personal issues that lurk within themselves.

The term 'wayfinder' is at first somewhat curious. Its use is intended to signal that the people in this faith position have found something of a way forward in their faith. I am also incorporating the journey motif that has been part of each of these faith positions to signal that the Integrated Wayfinders may be able to point to ways forward for those best characterized as Reflective Exiles or Transitional Explorers.

An interdependent faith

Disillusioned Followers	Reflective Exiles	Transitional Explorers	Integrated Wayfinders
Dependent relationship	Counter-dependency	Inner-dependency	**Inter-dependency**

During this phase the strongly focused inner-dependency of faith begins to allow more room for the company of others. Here the person desires to connect with individuals and groups of people of like faith and people of differing beliefs rather than be confined to one specific group. For Tim and Karen this meant a return to church. The church they joined was, however, quite different from the one they had left. The decision to become participants in a church again was the culmination of a number of factors. First, Tim and Karen's children were entering their early teenage years and as parents they wanted to provide their children with the opportunity of joining a church youth group and so find their own faith. Second, the couple themselves were experiencing a desire to meet with others who shared their faith.

> *Tim* We were thinking, 'Well, what about the kids?' The thought occurred to me that although the church are all wackos, I still couldn't deny the fact that there were people in churches who were Christians, who I felt a lot more affinity for than those close friends I might have had at work who weren't Christians. I realized I had an affinity with people who thought about Christ and considered themselves Christians, or identified with them. And I started to feel the need in myself to be recognized by a group of people who recognized Christ, that I could be recognized again as a fellow believer. So I could sort of speak my faith in fellowship with a wider body, at a club.[1]

The final factor that helped Tim and Karen rejoin a church after two years of not being part of one was the way the minister and the church in general functioned. They found they were warmly welcomed without pressure and yet given opportunities to be involved, almost immediately, in areas that interested them. The main difference from their old church was the 'sensible' government practices of the church,[2] where power was spread throughout the church community and people were free to disagree, to question and to argue about things without being shut down by the leadership. The church body also reflected a wide range of theological positions and was not dominated by evangelical or charismatic understandings and practices. Not all of the people I interviewed were able to find a church like Tim and Karen's. Denis and his family were unable to find a church as accommodating, but Denis has kept on going, albeit very much on the margins of the church. He and his wife wanted their two children to have a Christian faith background and so they continue to attend on Sundays.

> *Denis* I'm not interested. For quite a period of time, I found myself quite reactionary inside myself to what was going on.[3] It was just like the old scenarios being trotted out every Sunday. The old scenarios for the old guard and all that sort of stuff. And it just seemed so irrelevant to faith in real life. Just none of the essence of what it means to be fully human, which seems to be catered to in that church setting. You must be nice!

Explaining why he no longer feels comfortable in a church, Denis says:

> *Denis* It just seems to be stuck in a time warp and it doesn't move from where it actually is, and anything that does move through it and happens to move beyond it is then viewed with suspicion rather than the conception that you are actually on a journey of maturing faith and so forth. So basically now I am not reactionary any more, because I have got over that, and I just sit there and think about other things, really.

Although Denis finds the church environment unhelpful and something he simply bears for the sake of his children and family stability, he does connect with some groups of faith that help to nurture him. Denis is part of a Catholic spirituality prayer group which he finds 'deeply nurturing'. He is an infrequent attender at another more theologically broad-minded church which he finds 'theologically stimulating' and he and his wife are part of a small group of 'disaffected, post-institutional church people, who are very interested in authentic, fully human faith, and exploring issues. We meet every second week and we have found ourselves pretty comfortable there.'[4]

Alongside this, Denis has retained a strong inner-dependence for the nurture of his faith. 'For me at this stage of my faith pilgrimage, my faith is self-sustaining, by and large. I am still doing my own reading and I have my own practice of communing with God and all that sort of stuff. So I am quite self-sustaining in all that.'

The first characteristic of the integrative faith is therefore a new interdependence on both inner nurture for the life of faith and renewed connections with others who also provide the individual with nourishment and support in their faith. The new networks into which they connect represent a wider diversity of belief, values and expectations than the church they left previously. Making renewed connections with other groups of faith provides for the individual a context in which to contribute to others' lives or the life of a community. The desire to contribute, support and give to others is a growing desire among the Integrated Wayfinders.

An integrated faith

Disillusioned Followers	Reflective Exiles	Transitional Explorers	Integrated Wayfinders
Dependent relationship Received faith	Counter-dependency Deconstruction of faith	Inner-dependency Reconstruction of faith	Inter-dependency **Integrated faith**

The term 'integrated' is useful in drawing our attention to the 'completed, whole' faith system held by people at this stage and also to indicate the fully orbed nature of their faith. The integrated people have found, or more correctly built up for themselves, an understanding of their faith which is not reductionist or simplistic but which provides a coherent faith system and therefore a strong basis for their world view. In my interview with Denis he raised a number of issues critical to the basis of the EPC faith that he had questioned, reflected upon and found he could no longer hold to. For example, at one point he said:

> *Denis* Why have we got immune systems built into us genetically if before the fall[5] there was no disease? Well, God put them there because he knew it was going to happen. If God knew it was going to happen, he is a damn macabre person. Why the hell did Jesus have to die? Because God knew we were going to sin? No! God didn't know we were going to sin, he made it perfectly, and then – 'Oh shit, what can I do? Excuse me Jesus, can you pop

down there and hop on the cross? We have got to sort this blimmin' thing out, I didn't think of that one.' It is just expediency; it makes God thick or macabre, it doesn't work.

For Denis this problem required a great deal of study and thought until he found some answers in some ancient Christian theology and a liberationist interpretation of the Old Testament book of Job. He describes the process:

> *Denis* You can sit in church with reductionist answers, but your heart can't be in them any more so you have to find out, so you start going on this journey and there are answers. That is the wonderful thing. There are people out there who are thinking about it . . . this damn dude has written a book that is only that thick [*holding his hands up to show the spine of a book*[6] *less than a centimetre wide*] but it kicks your heart like nothing. You can trust this stuff, it's biblical, you can see it on the pages of the book. It is coherent. It is not all this bloody dualism, and it is utterly real in terms of your own heart suffering and the issues of the world and the struggles of the world. And it fires on all cylinders.

The building of a coherent faith system is one hallmark of those in this phase. Second, people here are building a fully orbed faith. By the use of this term I am drawing attention to a faith that incorporates and is relevant to all aspects of their lives. Helen, Rob's wife, says:

> *Helen* If your heart's right, every single day people come across your path where you make a choice of either to make their day better by some act, word or deed of yours, or to have no impact on their life because you're following your own agenda. And that happens every single day of your life. I think, to me, that's being close to God. It's not only how I speak to my husband and kids, how I live out my wifehood, motherhood, but how I speak to the person in the shop.

It is a faith that, as she says, has to be as relevant in the laundry as it is in the church. Rob chips in at this point, again moving forward in his chair with the air of someone about to make an important point: 'I see so many Christians who talk about worshipping God but they are oblivious to the fact that they are ecologically a cancer on the planet . . . I say you can't worship God on a Sunday morning and desecrate this planet all through the week. It is a total incongruity, it's an inconsistency that the church is oblivious to.' His reading in the area of ecology is for him 'food for the soul'. Tim and Karen talk about a minister Tim worked with who always spoke about the family having to come first, be the top priority in ministry, but who never lived like that. For Tim and Karen, this lack of an authentic faith is one aspect of what drove them to leave the church and seek to build a lifestyle that reflects their faith and a faith that reflects their lifestyle.

An autonomous faith

Disillusioned Followers	Reflective Exiles	Transitional Explorers	Integrated Wayfinders
Dependent relationship Received faith	Counter-dependency Deconstruction of faith	Inner-dependency Reconstruction of faith	Inter-dependency Integrated faith
Unexamined faith	Ongoing reflection	Emerging self-ownership	**Autonomous faith**

The third characteristic of the integrated faith is the autonomous or self-owned nature of people's faith at this point. Talking to people in this group leaves the discerning listener with no doubt about the personalized nature of their faith. It is a faith that is self-governed. The level of commitment and functionality of this faith for these people is very high. Rob and Denis exemplify this personal ownership of faith in the following comments.

Denis My commitment to Christian faith and my commitment to Christ is something that is prior to everything else in my experience, and exists independent of church, and it exists sort of independent of anything else in a lot of ways . . . So for me the integration of who I am in my personhood actually subsists in this whole way of looking at life, and reality which is Christ-centred. That might sound a bit amorphous. But everybody has a metaphysic, everybody actually functions out of a metaphysic, a view of what reality is. That experience, whole person, whole mind, whole metaphysic. What I am trying to say is that it is so deeply integrated as to how I sense myself to be.

Interviewer So you couldn't walk away from it?

Denis No, never! And not just because I did it so I have got to keep it up, because, hell's teeth, what else is there? But I found immense fruitfulness in my own sense of personhood and my own capacity to relate societally around issues, my own capacity to relate to people. My own capacity to live moment by moment daily life, out of a Christ-centred spirituality.

Rob I think my faith now is far more personally profound than it's ever been. I have faced doubts at the end, at the short end of a gun as it were, twice in the last few months. And I've done it with complete confidence and faith. I've been quite prepared to die with a good understanding of the character of God. And I've felt no fears of, 'Goodness, what a bummer of a time to have a heart attack! Just as you've left church, you know; thrown away the winning ticket.' I have not felt like that. I have felt total confidence that I am closer to God now than I have ever been, even though I've pulled away from all the things I'm supposed to do.

Linked with this new ownership is the ability to make articulate and clear definitions of what they believe[7] and how that may differ from the church environment within which they previously existed. Michelle and her husband Stuart went through some major health difficulties with their children which have been instrumental in a crisis of faith for Michelle. During this crisis, but also for a number of other reasons, they left the church they were very heavily involved in and formed a group to look at their faith and how it related to their real life issues. When I interviewed Michelle she summed up her faith in the following paragraph.

Michelle What is my faith and who do I believe? I came down to the nuts and bolts and said I do believe . . . I believe him to be good and true and holy and pure and loving . . . at this stage like Job I had laid my hand on my mouth and am having nothing much to say. Because he's bigger than I thought he was, I feel I need to get to know him in a much bigger way. Part of my journey now is to accept that I am here. And process my thoughts . . . usually telling him in my musings, thoughts and feelings . . . I feel sobered in my spirit . . . might be grief . . . I've been changed somehow.

A strong faith

Disillusioned Followers	Reflective Exiles	Transitional Explorers	Integrated Wayfinders
Dependent relationship	Counter-dependency	Inner-dependency	Inter-dependency
Received faith	Deconstruction of faith	Reconstruction of faith	Integrated faith
Unexamined faith	Ongoing reflection	Emerging self-ownership	Autonomous faith
Bold	Hesitant	Strengthening	**Strong**

The faith of the Integrated Wayfinders takes on a similar convictional strength to that expressed by Disillusioned Followers. The central difference, however, is between the unquestioning boldness of the Disillusioned Followers and the quiet strength and confidence of the Integrated Wayfinders. Here people have a new willingness to use their time, energy, skills and resources in pursuit of their faith. In a number of cases I met people who were making very large decisions or personal sacrifices as part of an outworking of their faith and in support of the communities of faith to which they are attached. For example, one couple was considering full-time work in a liturgical–mainstream church denomination, and another couple was considering travelling overseas to be involved in a restorationist church in Europe. Others were committing large amounts of time and money in the outworking of their faith in the wider community, either through an extension of their normal work or with voluntary organizations.

A number were investing time and energy in spiritual direction or spirituality groups, reading and study or continued reflection and prayer. As Rob said, he was throwing all his mental resources into the issue of the future of the church and Christian faith today. Rob did six units of theological study as well as working full-time the year prior to my interview with him. This occurred during a difficult personal year for him and his family. These units included two on other religions. Each of these people in their own different way engages in their faith through their time, their study, their interaction with others and their support and care of others.

Future involvement of the Integrated Wayfinders in the church

Rob talked of how the EPC church is inherently flawed. In doing so he drew my attention to the analogy in the New Testament of the world being like a harvest field that is ripe and ready for the picking. Rob suggests that in the evangelical church we have a reaping-centred Christianity but we don't know what to do with people as they mature in their Christian faith. He was therefore suggesting that EPC-type churches are strong on evangelism but comparatively weak in their emphasis on faith maturation.

> *Rob* We know how to cut them down [the ripe harvests] but we don't know how to stack them into sheaves and take the sheaves into the haystack. And we don't know what to do with the stuff then. We don't know how to get the ears of wheat off it and turn it into bread. All they are able to do is mow the harvest, so the whole experience of church growth is one of someone who goes out with a message and ultimately they do not bring anyone beyond their own experience – they just dilute the church to death. They've put themselves in the centre of a collection of perpetual spiritual babies. The role and the whole thrust of the church is to prepare gallons of spiritual milk just to keep those people coming back week after week. They never expect to take them beyond that childhood stage to a place where the people are independent of the leaders.

For the reflective faith person this kind of church environment causes an almost intolerable sense of confinement, where their concerns, questions, doubts and growing edges are not acknowledged or often even tolerated. In a confused, sometimes angry state they leave this kind of church as their world view which had been based on their faith comes into disarray. Transitional people, on the other hand, are beginning to identify some faith struts that they can rely on as foundational pieces in a new faith system.

For a number of the integrated faith people the structures of the EPC churches are also difficult to coexist easily within. According to their depiction, the focus of these churches on evangelism rather than spiritual development, on exuberant rather than reflective forms of worship, on prayer that is demanding or coercive in its approach rather than a meditative listening to God, on the cognitive aspects of the faith rather than people's experience of God or their feelings, and on hierarchical structures of leadership and control rather than more open inclusive forms of decision-making, all serve to alienate the integrated faith person.

Despite the difficulties, each of the integrated faith people interviewed had made some connections with people, groups or churches that hold to similar beliefs and a similar faith. The degree to which they will build ongoing strong connections with these people, groups and churches will be dependent on the openness of these communities to people like themselves and the degree to which they can overcome some of the weaknesses at this point of the faith journey.

A dynamic process

The major categories of leavers described here may appear to make a very fluid and dynamic process seem like an ordered and sequential movement from one box to another. For the interviewees involved, the process is anything but a neat jumping from box to box. It is, as one person described it, like being 'adrift on the sea', tossed by the ocean waves, blown by the changing winds and pulled by the hidden currents. The person moves this way and that, perhaps more aware of an overall turbulence than any clear directional path. It is often only in hindsight that interviewees discern the trajectory they have travelled and are able to make sense of both their journey and their faith.

NOTES

1 For Tim and Karen the church was likened to a club. Tim said that he realized that he was a cricketer and his work friends all played rugby and he wanted to meet with some cricketers again. So they joined a sensible cricket club. The way Tim and Karen approached this decision is indicative of this. They said that they sat down and worked out what the fees would be (i.e. what they would need to contribute financially as participants) and decided that it was worth it and joined up.

2 The church Tim and Karen have joined can be described as an evangelical Anglican church (this is how a leader within the church characterized it).

The church is made up of people from a wide variety of theological streams including evangelicals, charismatics and liberals. The church does not try to cater exclusively to any one of these groups but attempts to include all of them. The sensible government was also expressed, in Tim's mind, in the way anyone can disagree publicly with a previous speaker (regardless of who that person is – including the minister).

3 Denis's use of the word 'reactionary' should be read as something he reacted to within himself rather than as a personality characteristic.

4 In many ways the relationship between the Integrated Wayfinders and the church is like that described in Thornton Wilder's classic *Our Town*, where 'the young wife Emily dies in childbirth. Given the right to return to some special day of her life, she goes back to a birthday she remembers as a child. When she returns she sees her familiar loved ones going about their ordinary routines, but they cannot see her nor do they see the terrible beauty visible to her from beyond the grave. She flees, glad to return where the pain is at least bearable.' Here Loren Mead comments that 'Wilder has given us a portrayal of what it is like to have awakened into a new paradigm and how hard it is to communicate with those still living in the old one' (quoted in Mead, 1993, p. 22).

5 'The fall' is here used as a label for the emergence of evil in the world as presented in Genesis (the first book of the Bible). In the Genesis account, evil and sin enter the world through the choices of the man and the woman in the garden to eat the one fruit that God had told them not to eat. This incident is called 'the fall'.

6 A commentary on the book of Job.

7 For example Denis, talking about his beliefs, said: 'I am still evangelical, the evangel, the gospel, personal commitment to Christ, death and resurrection, bodily resurrection and all the deity and humanity, trinity all the basic credal stuff I have no difficulty with . . . in a Baptist setting, there are the conservative evangelical churches which are very blinkered. I am wanting to throw the blinkers off and spread it wider. But from the majority of Baptist church settings I'm liberal. [*Laughs*] It is all relative, but you can see what I'm getting at. I'm classed as a liberal. I am not fundamentalist and I'm not Pentecostal. But I am thoroughly evangelical.'

EIGHT

Bringing it all together . . . where's the map?

Imagine going to a beach for the first time and observing people swimming and playing in the water. They seem to be enjoying themselves enormously and are obviously proficient at swimming. After a while you get to know some of the swimmers and they offer to teach you to swim so you too can enjoy the water. Seeing what they have encourages you to join them. Swimming turns out to be a great success and for the next few years you enjoy swimming at the beach as part of the club. Eventually you become a swimming instructor yourself. You are challenged by the opportunity to help others learn to swim between the flags and enjoy the sea as you have learnt to do.

One day standing on the beach you wonder what it would be like to swim further, to go exploring the rock edges, or maybe to dive to the depths of the bay out beyond the flags. The yearning to stretch out beyond the beach doesn't simply go away but appears to get stronger and builds within you. Around the same time you notice that you are becoming increasingly self-conscious about going swimming. It doesn't seem as important, or as much of a challenge as it used to. Thinking about this makes you realize you don't enjoy the swimming club like you used to and you're becoming critical of all the swimming and playing near the beach. But then socializing with a group of deep-sea fishermen each weekend and hearing their stories of fishing trips adds fuel to your desire to go beyond the flags. As time drifts on, dislike turns to resentment and you tentatively mention to some of the others at the beach your desire to go beyond the flags. The coach gets to hear of your comments and warns you of the dangers of swimming outside the flags. He tells stories of people who went out there and have never come back. Instead he suggests that you go to a swim-meet to rekindle your enthusiasm.

The swim-meet seems to do the trick at least for a while, but then standing on the beach one day the yearnings return, this time even stronger than before. On swimming days you find it harder and harder to get yourself out of bed and are aware of making all sorts of excuses as to why you shouldn't swim that day. One swimming day you wake up realizing you haven't been to the beach for three or four months. You wonder what to do next. Should you go back or not? Eventually you come to the conclusion you don't ever want to go back again. All you do there is swim backwards and forwards and play in the waves. It was fun, even exciting for a number of years and you thought swimming was all there was to life, but not now. Now you want more. Of course, you remain a swimmer; after all, no one can deny your experience of the sea. But you're rarely seen at the beach between the flags.

For many EPC church leavers, this story has a high degree of resonance with their own faith journey. They too end up leaving a 'club' that has been very important to them and significant in the formation of who they are as people. Leaving brings with it a mix of feelings and reactions; partly a resentment, disinterest or critique of the style of church they have been involved in and yet at the same time a sense of loss and a desire to go on to something else.

As Jake put it:

Jake My moment of truth happened a couple of years ago. It was Sunday morning, I was in church. A preacher, visiting from another city, was giving the sermon. I was bored, impatiently waiting for him to finish, so that I could go home. As a regular church attender for over 15 years, I had heard a lot of sermons. Lately, however, I was finding that almost all these messages seemed strangely irrelevant and unconnected to the issues in life that were important to me.[1]

This would be Jake's last time at the church. Prior to this particular morning he had assumed that the cause of his disinterest and boredom was within himself, thinking he was 'backsliding' or at the very least complacent. However, on this Sunday morning he realized, 'If there was a problem, it might not just be in me.' Jake quickly found that he was not alone in the feelings he had. Explaining his journey with others often seemed to elicit an enthusiastic response of, 'Yes, that's exactly how I feel!' This led him to explore in more depth what lay behind these feelings. Because of his extensive training in human psychological development, Jake was aware of developmental theories that explained how people move through successive stages in their processes of thinking, ethical decision-making and understandings of life and the world.

Further reading led him to the work of James Fowler, a professor of theology and human development and also an ordained minister of the United Methodist Church of America. In this work on the stages of faith development, Fowler outlined a series of typical faith stages through which people move as their faith matures. He showed how the transition between these stages can often be traumatic and involved, leaving behind some of the elements of the previous stage. What Fowler was describing made sense to Jake both as a professional in human psychological and physiological development, but perhaps more importantly it connected with his own changing faith and his changing relationship with the Pentecostal church he belonged to.

Of course, what Fowler points to in his six stages has been known by generations of Christians. Many of the writings of the Christian saints of old indicate a similar progression of Christian faith involving distinct changes and stages. St Teresa of Avila, in her account of the Christian journey as a progression through different rooms of the Interior Castle, describes a very similar process to that of Fowler's faith stages. There are more examples in the writings of the Catholic spiritual leaders like St John of the Cross and St Thomas Aquinas. But it isn't only the great Catholic spiritual leaders who wrote about faith stages. In story form so did John Bunyan in the classic novel *Pilgrim's Progress* and Hannah Hurnard in her novel *Hinds' Feet on High Places*. For previous generations of Christians, and Christians within other streams of the church, such writings were well known and the progressions they describe have been generally accepted. In the EPC churches, concerned to deal with fact, not fiction and segregated from the writings of the Catholic spiritual directors, there is often little mention and even less understanding of the idea of faith stages and of faith being a journey with normal, even predictable crises and change points.

The great strength of the evangelical church is its focus on conversion. Bebbington describes the evangelical movement as being founded on four core principles. One of these is what he calls 'conversionism', a focus on helping and leading people to make a conscious choice to follow Jesus Christ. James Fowler appreciates the significance of conversion as a crucial aspect of the Christian journey, stating in one of his later books that: 'Our first concern, of course, is the proclamation of the gospel and the attempt to help it find a deep and firm rooting in the soil of people's lives' (Fowler, 1987, p. 81). However, he also goes further, suggesting that the journey of Christian faith is built on not one but two processes which taken together constitute what he calls the 'dance of faith development in our lives'. These two processes are conversion and development. Conversion involves the transformation and intensification of faith. Faith development is the slower, less radical maturing and evolving of faith similar to the physical process of human maturation. For Fowler faith development occurs through the ongoing dance of faith involving these twin movements of radical conversion and gradual maturation. Both are integral and necessary movements. Within the evangelical movement the emphasis on one movement of the dance – conversion – has led to a reduced understanding of and focus on the second movement of the dance – faith development. Although evangelical churches have been strong on discipleship, especially immediately after conversion, this has generally not lead to an ongoing focus on the maturing of Christian faith, particularly in terms of major faith transitions and changes.

Meeting with and listening to the accounts of church leavers, both as part of my research and subsequently in our group Spirited Exchanges, I have been struck by how almost exclusively these people, on reflection, see their leaving as a moving on, a next step, something they feel drawn to do. Fowler's analysis and the previous descriptions of Christian life by the historical Catholic leaders and Christian novelists help us to explain this and to understand such changes as part of a 'normal Christian life'.

In the following section I want to introduce a map of faith development described by Fowler in his staged faith theory. In order to do this I will introduce his theory and then outline the relevant adult faith stages involved. I have found that for many people there is a revelatory 'ahh' experience in seeing this material for the first time.

Fowler's stages of faith

Although there are other faith development theories available that could be used, I am focusing our attention on Fowler's theory for a number of reasons. First, Fowler is the leading theorist in the area – his key publication on faith development, *Stages of Faith: The Psychology of Human Development and the Quest for Meaning*[2] has gone through more than 50 reprints and sold in excess of 230,000 copies worldwide. Second, Fowler's theory has been extensively investigated in hundreds of faith stage interviews, in cross-cultural analysis, and in numerous critiques and debates in academic psychological journals, theological journals and in local congregations. Third, although Fowler's theory is now over 20 years old it remains the most significant work in the field. Finally, Fowler as a Christian and theologian was able to draw heavily on Christian theology in the development of the theory as well as on his own professional discipline of psychology.

Like any map, Fowler's stages of faith describes the terrain and shows key landmarks. However, as anyone who has tramped can appreciate, a map, although very useful, often doesn't depict the terrain as it really is. Bush country that on the map looks easy to move through is often impossible to penetrate in real life. Hills that look easy to climb on the map may be unassailable on the ground. No doubt we can all identify with the track which looks like an easy half-hour stroll on the map but in reality takes hours of sweaty determination to complete. While the stages of faith do provide a map, it is a very scant one. Everyone's journey through life, and especially their own journey of faith, is distinct and unique. Where a general map can provide some key markers and a description of other people's journeys it cannot spell out the specific detail of anyone's personal journey.

In describing the way Fowler's theory can be used as a map I have come to see it as a bare-bones kind of map. There are many different types of maps: topographical maps, which give precise details of an area; road maps, which give less detail and are somewhat stylized; and the maps printed in tourist pamphlets that are heavily stylized and indicate only a few general markers. Using this analogy, the faith stage map is like the map at the back of a tourist brochure; helpful but certainly not detailed or authoritative.

In introducing Fowler's stages of faith as a bit of a map for many people's faith journeys we need to be aware of a few of the introductory comments that Fowler makes about his theory of faith stages. First, for Fowler faith has to be viewed as a dynamic, changing and evolving process; not as something relatively static. For this reason he sees faith as a verb. Grammatically and in normal conversation we think of faith as a noun – something you have or don't have. But Fowler understands faith as a verb, a process of becoming, involving our loving, trusting, believing, acting, suffering, valuing, knowing and committing. In this sense faith is more than acceptance of certain statements of belief – it is a way of living which encompasses all of life.

Second, Fowler's stages focus more on the *how* we believe (what he calls the operations of faith) than the *what* we believe (the contents of our faith). In fact people often hold the same beliefs at different faith stages. What changes at each stage is their understanding, experience and the out-working of these particular beliefs. Specifically Fowler suggests that change at each stage occurs in the following areas:

1 The way people think;
2 Their ability to see another's point of view;
3 The way they arrive at moral judgements;
4 The way and extent to which they draw boundaries around their faith community;
5 The way they relate to external 'authorities' and their truth claims;
6 The way they form their world view; and
7 The way they understand and respond to symbols. (Richter and Francis, 1998, p. 53)

Although Fowler outlines six stages we need to remember that very few people progress through all six; many only progress through the first two or three. Because of this Fowler is very careful to ensure that no stage is seen as better than another. People who settle (what he calls 'equilibrate') at one stage do not have a better faith nor are they more saved than someone who is best described as being at another faith stage. Yet despite Fowler's insistence that no stage is higher or better than another, there is a sense in which each stage offers a deeper and broader understanding and experience of faith than the stage which precedes it.

The faith journey that Fowler describes is not a gentle undemanding stroll through life, involving gradual and imperceptible steps. On the contrary, the transitions between stages are often experienced as radical upheavals and major crises. Sharon Parks, who also writes in the area of faith development, likens the whole faith stage transition to being shipwrecked.

> To undergo shipwreck is to be threatened in a most total and primary way. Shipwreck is the coming apart of what has served as shelter and protection and has held and carried one where one wanted to go – the collapse of a structure that once promised trustworthiness. Likewise, when we undergo the shipwreck of meaning at the level of faith, we feel threatened at the very core of our existence. (Parks, 1986, p. 24)

We need to be aware that such transitional changes can be very difficult for the person involved and it may seem quite literally as though their faith is shipwrecked. This feeling can carry on for long periods of time, often years rather than months. Because the transition stage means enduring the dissolution of a total way of making sense of things, it frequently includes living with fundamental ambiguity and a deep sense of alienation. These faith stage transitions can be so difficult, painful and protracted that people often remain fixed in a previous stage rather than face the difficulty or uncertainty of transition. In fact, people tend to stay where they are until the pain of staying where they are becomes unbearable.

Having outlined some of the background to Fowler's stages of faith we can now begin to traverse the descriptions of each stage. The titles I will use for each stage are taken from Charles McCullough's book *Heads of Heaven; Feet of Clay.* Although these are not the titles that Fowler gives them they do give a clearer and more readily memorable summary of the core features of each stage. Fowler's own titles for each stage are included in brackets.

STAGE I – THE INNOCENT (INTUITIVE–PROJECTIVE)
This stage is found in pre-school children whose lives are a seamless world of fantasy, stories, experiences and imagery. Their experience of God and faith is understood through the family experience. Where parents talk about God and pray with the children or say grace, some understand-

ing begins to develop, but at this stage there are no inner structures with which to sort their experiences. Life is therefore a collage of disorganized images including real events of daily life and the imaginary fantasy life of the child. The transition to the next stage involves the child's growing concern to know how things are and to clarify what is real and what only seems that way (Fowler, 1995, pp. 125–34).

STAGE 2 – THE LITERALIST (MYTHICAL–LITERAL)
This stage normally begins when the child is around six years of age. Somewhere around this age the child is better able to organize their experiences and begin to categorize them. At this stage ideas and stories are interpreted literally, as the following conversation illustrates:

> *Debra* 'Daddy, where's God?'
> *Daddy* 'Honey, we believe that God is everywhere.'
> *Debra* 'Is God in this house, then?'
> *Daddy* 'Yes, dear, God is in this house.'
> *Debra* 'Daddy, is God in this room?'
> *Daddy* 'Well, yes, honey, I think God is in this room.'

Debra goes to the kitchen sink and takes a cup off the shelf, and points into it.

> *Debra* 'Then God is in this cup?'
> *Daddy* 'Yes, Debra. I think God is . . . in some ways . . . in that cup.'

Debra holds the cup in the air, eyeing it critically. Then quickly a smile crosses her face, she places her hand firmly across the top of the cup, and exults:

> *Debra* 'Goody! I've got him!' (Stokes, 1992, p. 16)

As this indicates, children at this stage interpret stories and adults' explanations of life and faith literally. They love the stories from the Bible about Noah's ark, Jonah and the whale or David and Goliath, often taking enormous interest in the details of the size of the ark, the number of animals or what it would have been like inside the whale. Although powerfully influenced by narrative and story, children at this stage cannot stand back and view events from the position of a neutral observer as they lack

113

the ability to reflect on their own position or the position of others from a value-free perspective.

During this second stage the bounds of the child's world widen. The primary influence of the family is now added to by the influence of teachers, school, other children, television, videos, films and books. Here the child typically makes strong associations with people like *us* and is aware and often critical of those who are different.

Although this stage begins in childhood, for many this is the stage at which their faith journey equilibrates during adulthood or at least for a substantial portion of their adulthood. M. Scott Peck, who utilizes a simplified form of Fowler's stages, suggests that from his experience about 20 per cent of the adult population may best be characterized at this stage of faith (Peck, 1993, p. 121). These adults tend to appreciate churches where a more literal interpretation of Scripture is encouraged. This stage brings with it real strengths, offering security for the individual and deep conviction and commitment.

Adults at this stage are often strongly influenced by rules and authoritative teaching, their main images of God tending to be of a stern and just, but loving parent.

STAGE 3 – THE LOYALIST (SYNTHETIC–CONVENTIONAL)
Stage three is a conformist stage in which the individual is 'acutely tuned to the expectations and judgements of significant others' (Fowler, 1995, p. 173). It is very much a tribal stage, where being part of the tribe is powerfully significant to the person. Here the security of the tribe or community of like-minded believers is important to the individual's own beliefs, values and faith. Loyalists may hold deep convictions and are often committed workers or servers who have a very strong sense of loyalty. While their beliefs and values are often deeply held they are typically not examined critically and are therefore tacitly held to. That is, they know what they know but are generally unable to tell you how they know something is true except by referring to an external authority outside of themselves. The most common examples of this are 'the Bible says so', or 'my pastor teaches this'.

At this stage the person has not stood outside their belief system and made a personal in-depth critique of it. They are, as George Santayana describes,

> analogous to the situation of the fish in a tank. Supported and sustained by water it has no means of leaping out of the aquarium so as to reflect on the tank and its contents. A person in stage three is aware of having values and normative images. He or she articulates them, defends them and feels deep emotional investments in them, but typically has not made the value system, as a system, the object of reflection. (Fowler, 1995, p. 161–2)

Predominantly these people have a vision of God as an external, transcendent being and in discussion refer little to God as an immanent in-dwelling God – what Quakers call the inner light. Perhaps because of this many are uncomfortable with the notion of the God within.

Among adults this is the stage most commonly found among church members. This should not be surprising, as this is why we have churches and congregations in which people can find some common faith identity, and a community of faith to which to belong, where the individual's beliefs, values and actions are shaped. Often identification with their church is a key identity marker for them. Most find enormous meaning for their faith as they share in the activities of the church – worship, teaching, prayer and mission endeavours. Many experience a strong sense of belonging to their church community, which is often expressed as having 'an arrived feel to it', being 'at home' and providing a 'walled-in' (Pressau, 1977) commitment. At this stage people tend to become dependent on the church community for confirmation of selfhood and faith. They will often work hard to provide support in times of trouble or difficulty in others' lives and to maintain a supportive web of relatedness. The image of the church community as a large family is often very appealing; people 'may feel a special gladness in thinking of the congregation as an intergenerational community bound together in friendship and shared experiences' (Fowler, 1987, p. 87). Because of this, conflict and controversy are threatening to them. They will tend to work for harmony and would often prefer to bury conflict than allow it to surface and potentially destabilize the sense of community that is so important to them.

This stage of faith is often expressed in dualistic understandings. Dualisms between good and bad, sacred and secular, Christian and non-Christian, saved and unsaved. Such dualisms provide a grid to locate both themselves and other people.

Fowler illustrates this stage with a drawing of the Loyalist surrounded by other key individuals. Here the individual is surrounded by the values, beliefs and convictions of significant others from their community. They are, as Fowler has identified, 'acutely attuned to the expectations and judgements of these significant others and as yet do not have a sure enough grasp of their own identity or faith in their own autonomous judgement to construct and maintain an independent perspective' (Fowler, 1995, p. 173).

STAGE 4 – THE CRITIC (INDIVIDUATIVE–REFLECTIVE)

The transition to the fourth stage of faith is probably the most difficult to traverse and involves the greatest dismantling of what was learnt and experienced in the previous stage. Because of the 'walled-in', secure feel of the third stage it often takes a major upset for the transition beyond stage three to begin. Fowler describes the move as a two-part transition. The first involves the emergence of a new sense of self that will take responsibility for its own actions, beliefs and values and will stand out against the significant others of the past. This is often a courageous and difficult journey. The second aspect is a new objectification and examination of the beliefs, values and expectations they have received.

Fowler illustrates this stage using a drawing in which the Critic stands alone outside of any group. It is clear in his illustration that the Critic has removed themself from the encircling relationship of significant others and is developing an independent position. At this stage the individual is increasingly uncomfortable with being asked to conform to the beliefs, teachings, values and actions of the group.

In their examination of their faith and practice, Critics begin by raising previously accepted beliefs, values, world views and actions for inspection, often as if they were looking at them and analysing them for the first time. In this critical examination flaws, inconsistencies, unanswered aspects and overly simplistic solutions seem to be their primary focus. This is a process of unpicking their previous faith and their communities' beliefs and practices. It is lonely, uncomfortable and often protracted.

116

But through this process a new respect and trust for one's inner feelings, intuitions and personal judgement is commonly experienced. In contrast to the previous stage, the Critic trusts their own perception more than the perception and view of any community of others.

People at this stage tend to hold themselves, and others, more accountable for their own 'authenticity, congruence, and consistency' (Fowler, in Fowler and Keen, 1985, p. 70). It is important to people that they take responsibility for their beliefs, actions and decisions. They will not tolerate following the crowd, or previously held significant others. Freedom to make their own decisions becomes increasingly important to them. Because of these changes the place of relationships changes too. No longer are relationships essential for the formation and maintenance of identity: this is a strongly individualistic stage. Where relationships are built a high priority is placed on each person's autonomous identity. As the stage progresses a person's reference group tends to widen enormously. The person becomes interested in the views, beliefs and practices of groups they may previously have stayed away from.

For Critics, symbols and rituals only continue to be significant if their content can be translated into usable concepts which carry meaning for the individual. That is, they can be accepted as illustrations of truth.

Where the stage four Critic may also be involved in groups, churches or congregations, they are looking for acknowledgement and support of their self-authorization. Groups that provide intellectual stimulation and challenge but do not try to impose external or conventional expectations and beliefs are most comfortable to people at this stage. They often appreciate forums which allow them to question, present divergent opinions and in which divergence of belief and practice is appreciated, even celebrated. They are now more comfortable with criticism and debate, even disagreement. The conflict and disagreement that was once seen as potentially threatening is now viewed more positively, perhaps even relished.

At this stage people frequently see themselves as 'self-sufficient, self-starters, self-managing and self-repairing' (Fowler, 1987, p. 91). Because of the strength of the sense of self and the inner determinacy, people at this stage do not sit easily within a leadership structure that requires them to be dependent. They want a leadership structure that acknowledges and respects their personal positions and allows room for them to contribute to the decision-making.

STAGE 5 – THE SEER[3] (CONJUNCTIVE)

This stage is not as easy to explain as the previous stage, as it encapsulates what seem contradictory aspects. In fact, it is this seeming contradiction that lies at the heart of stage five, for at this stage the firm boundaries of the previous stage become more porous. The confident self becomes humblingly aware of the depth of the unconscious and the unknown. This is a process that often coincides with a realization of the power and reality of death. Although the transition between stages can't be fixed to certain ages and people move through at different paces and equilibrate at different points, this stage is seldom reached before the onset of mid-life. Fowler sums up the prerequisite experience necessary for this stage by saying we have learnt 'by having our noses rubbed in our own finitude' (Fowler, 1987, p. 93).

Fowler describes this stage by outlining four distinctive hallmarks:

- An awareness of the need to face and hold together several unmistakable *polar tensions* in one's life: the polarities of being both *old* and *young* and of being both *masculine* and *feminine* . . . The polarity of having a conscious and a shadow self (Fowler, 1984, p. 65).
- A felt sense that truth is more multiform and complex than most of the clear, either/or categories of the previous stage. In its richness, ambiguity, and multidimensionality, truth must be approached from at least two or more angles of vision simultaneously (Fowler, 1984, p. 65).[4] People at this level will resist a forced synthesis or reductionist interpretation and are generally prepared to live with ambiguity, mystery, wonder and apparent irrationalities (Fowler, in Fowler and Keen, 1985, p. 81).
- Here faith moves beyond the reductive strategy by which the Critic interprets symbol, myth, and liturgy into conceptual meanings . . . The faith of the Seer gives rise to a second naïveté,[5] a postcritical receptivity and readiness for participation in the reality brought to expression in symbol and myth (Fowler, 1984, p. 65).
- A genuine openness to the truths of traditions and communities other than one's own. This openness, however, is not to be equated with a relativistic agnosticism (literally a not knowing), [for this stage of] faith exhibits a combination of committed belief in and through the

particularities of a tradition, while insisting upon the humility that knows that the grasp on ultimate truth that any of our traditions can offer needs continual correction and challenge (Fowler, 1984, pp. 65–6).

As Fowler's hallmarks of stage five suggest, people at this stage love mystery and seem to relish the vastness of the unknown. They seek to understand the great unknowns, realizing the more they understand, the more the unknown is opened up before them.

Here people are able to identify with perspectives other than their own. Many ex-EPC church people talked of a new discovery and appreciation of Catholic expressions of faith, others of gaining much from liberation theology, feminist theology, creation spirituality or aspects of the New Age movement. This does not involve an uncritical or total acceptance of these perspectives; rather it is an acknowledgement and incorporation within their own faith and understanding of a number of new perspectives.

The Seer's faith is clearly the Seer's own. Although nurtured by the faith of parents, significant leaders, writers and the lives of others it is the individual's own compilation and one that is deeply held. Their faith may well be quite orthodox, deviating little, if at all, from the faith espoused in EPC church communities, or it may relish aspects of faith and ideology from other perspectives. What is significant is that it is the owned and firmly rooted faith of the individual, a faith that shapes and connects with all aspects of their lives.

Because of the strength of their own stance, people at this stage are able to identify with people of different races, socio-economic status and different belief systems. In fact, such cross-cultural experiences are generally sought after and often important aspects of the individual's life and faith. The boundaries of faith at this stage are very broad and often difficult for others to identify. For this reason people at stage five are often confusing, irritating, even threatening to those at previous stages. As Fowler says, these individuals are 'not likely to be "true-believers", in the sense of an undialectical, single-minded, uncritical devotion to a cause or ideology . . . they know that the line between the righteous and the sinners goes through the heart of each of us and our communities, rather than between us and them' (Fowler, 1984, p. 67).

STAGE 6 — THE SAINT (UNIVERSALIZING)

The final stage is the most difficult to understand and is perhaps better described through poetry than by definitions. It involves two major transitions: first, what Fowler calls a 'decentration from self', in which the self is removed from the centre or focus of the individual's life. It is a move beyond the usual human obsessions with survival, security and significance coupled with a continued widening of the circle of 'those who count'. The second transition is a shift in motivation to the complete acceptance of the ultimate authority of God in all aspects of life. This shift is perhaps best illustrated when we observe Jesus in the garden of Gethsemane: 'Father, if thou art willing, remove this cup from me; nevertheless not my will, but thine, be done' (Luke 22.42, RSV).

The results of Fowler's own research indicated that only a small percentage of the population could be described as operating at this level. His findings showed only 1.6 per cent of those 61 years of age and over who were interviewed operated at this faith stage. Of all the people Fowler interviewed under 61 years of age not one was identified as being at this stage. In my own interviews I found only one person who could be described as operating at the sixth stage. Fowler gives the following examples: Mother Teresa, Dietrich Bonhoeffer and Martin Luther King. These are people of a rare faith quality encapsulated in the title 'Saint'.

Stages of faith and groups

These stages not only apply to individuals but also to families, churches and other societal groups. Fowler suggests that as an individual can be described as operating at a particular faith stage so too can a group of people, a family, a church and a given societal group. To explain this, Fowler discusses the average acceptable level of faith development for adults in a given community (Fowler, 1995, p. 294). In EPC churches the teaching, worshipping patterns, styles of governance and esteemed role models are predominantly pitched at Fowler's third stage of faith development.

We are now able to consider more fully one of the core questions relating to church leavers. Why do some people move on through the stages of faith while others become stable long-term residents at particular points? Fowler suggests three things can be significant influences in disrupting a person's faith position and encouraging them to move further along the stages. Suffering – especially intense and ongoing personal suffering – can provide the necessary stimulus for some. Education that gives people the tools to question, analyse and search for alternative understandings and vantage points can also be significant. Perhaps the most significant, though, is being exposed to an environment that encourages the next faith stage transition.

In the analogy that began this chapter, the swimmer felt a sense of internal dissatisfaction with swimming between the flags. This was encouraged by spending time with the deep-sea fishermen, hearing their stories of fishing trips and experiences beyond the bay. In the same way the internal desire of many to move beyond their present faith understandings, practices and experiences is sponsored by engaging in other contexts where further exploration, personal growth and the pursuit of truth in all its complexity is expected and modelled.

The decision to leave for most of the church leavers was a mix of three essential ingredients. All three need to be present before an individual who has been strongly committed and involved in their church community is ready or able to move out. First there needs to be an internal desire to move beyond the faith stage presently reached. Second there needs to be an external context that is able to sponsor the internal desire of this individual. Examples of these sponsoring contexts may be prolonged periods of suffering, higher education or perhaps engaging in a particular work, social or relational grouping. The final essential ingredient is being immersed in a church that through its teaching, worship, governance patterns and accepted role models discourages people from exploring the faith stages that their own internal desire and external context are fostering.

Where an individual is engaged both in a church community that is constraining the shift to later faith stages and a wider cultural context that is sponsoring such a shift, a dilemma is set up. For many people the internal desire to move beyond the comfort of the third stage of faith sponsored by their involvement in the wider cultural context encourages them to end up leaving the faith-constraining environment of their church.

121

The leavers I have met consistently described a context of work, study, friendships or family that encouraged and sponsored their exploration beyond the accepted faith stage of their church. To go through the internal dislocation of one comfortable lived-out experience of faith and move into new unknown areas, people need a convergence of an internal personal need coupled with the sponsoring and encouraging support of an external context.

Fowler goes on to suggest that many aspects of the emerging postmodernist society act as sponsors encouraging people engaged in this emerging culture to the later stages of faith development. He points to the postmodern culture's openness to doubt and questions, willingness to critique and ability to see truth as a complex paradox. Added to this is postmodernity's focus on relational networks rather than impersonal institutions and the emerging culture's emphasis on a desire to learn through participation, experiences and dialogue. The postmodern culture therefore provides an ideal environment to sponsor adults beyond the third stage of faith and into the stage of the Critic. Here Fowler is suggesting that adults who engage positively with the emerging postmodernist culture are therefore being exposed to a context that sponsors the move into the fourth and fifth stages of faith.

As the influence of the postmodernist culture takes a stronger and stronger hold, such leave-taking can only increase. This implies that for a growing number of people who are comfortable in an increasingly postmodernist society, many EPC churches are going to be seen as personally faith-limiting environments.

Figure 8.1 joins the diagrammatic progression of the different groups of church leavers and the stages of faith described by Fowler to show how the different groups of EPC church leavers connect with the faith stages. In this diagram the EPC church is aligned to Fowler's third stage of faith. This is because EPC churches through their structures, beliefs and faith packages, and particularly their public teaching, worship, and governance patterns encourage adults to become settled at this third stage. While clearly a number of individuals within EPC churches do move to the fourth and fifth stages of faith, this is not the dominant stage portrayed in the public practices of EPC churches. In using this diagram we need to remember that the personal journey is a dynamic and fluid process,

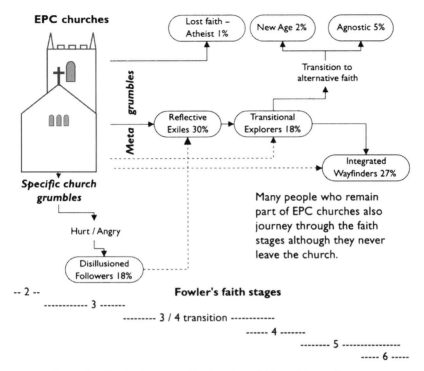

Figure 8.1 Fowler's stages of faith and the faith positions of leavers

and while the diagram shows a neat progression from one category to another it fails to show the complexity, struggle and fluid motion which is the experience of real faith journeyers.

This understanding of the journey takes us back to the analogy of swimming in the ocean. The map helps to make sense of the yearning of the swimmer to go beyond the flags. Such a feeling is not a giving up of the desire to be in the sea but a yearning to move into new depths, a yearning that can only be satisfied by going beyond the flags. Reading about the experiences of others who have explored further beyond the safe shallows will not suffice. Each individual who experiences this deep longing is drawn to go to the depths themselves. Intuitively they know that the treasures of the deep can only be personally collected. The treasures of others who have learned to dive may be encouraging but they can never satisfy the need to pick up one's own treasures from the bottom of the bay personally.

Having moved beyond the flags and tried to dive and explore the depths, one becomes aware of the vagaries of the ocean. In the water beyond the flags, different rules apply. Immersed in water one could easily drown. New ways of moving in the deep need to be found, new equipment mastered and whole new sets of knowledge gained. There are totally new dangers – pressure, currents, reduced visibility and empty oxygen tanks. It is an experience that typically brings with it a new respect and awe, a recognition that the words of the coach held a great deal of truth – it is dangerous beyond the flags. But this is not a danger that needs to be stayed away from. It is a danger that means you can't be blasé or too self-assured. The experience of diving brings a new awareness of the need for new skills and a respect for experienced divers. In fact, the deeper we go the more we are aware of the risks, the need for much greater skill and experienced companions. Yet coupled with this is a greater understanding and respect for the ocean itself – its breadth and depth, changing faces, deep mysteries, vastness and rich treasures. Like the ocean, so it is with God: risk and respect, treasures and threats, experience and understanding grow the deeper one goes.

NOTES

1 Unpublished paper by church leaver.
2 First published in 1981.
3 Fowler titles this stage the 'Conjunctive stage'. The name can be traced to Nicholas of Cusa (1401–64), whose greatest work, *De Docta Ignorantia*, developed the idea of God as the *coincidentia oppositorum* – the coincidence of opposites – the being wherein all opposites and contradictions meet and are reconciled. Carl Jung adapted this idea in many of his psychological writings on religion, altering the term to the *coniunctio oppositorum* – the conjunction of opposites (Fowler, in Fowler and Keen, 1985, p. 79).
4 Fowler goes on to illustrate this point with reference to a scientific example: 'Like the discovery in physics that to explain the behaviour of light requires two different and irreconcilable models – one based on the model of packets of energy and one based on wave theory' (Fowler, 1984, p. 65).
5 Fowler explains the concept of second naïveté, stating: 'In Paul Ricoeur's powerful language, Conjunctive faith is not to be equated with a "first naï-

veté", a pre-critical relationship of unbroken participation in symbolically mediated reality. That style more aptly describes Stage 3 Synthetic–Conventional faith. Conjunctive faith has experienced the breaking of its symbols and the "vertigo of relativity". It is a veteran of critical reflection and of the effort to "reduce" the symbolic, the liturgical and the mythical to conceptual meanings . . . Ricoeur's term "second naïveté" or "willed naïveté" begins to describe Conjunctive faith's post-critical desire to resubmit to the initiative of the symbolic. It decides to do this, but it has to relearn how to do this. It carries forward the critical capacities and methods of the previous stage, but it no longer trusts them except as tools to avoid self-deception and to order truths encountered in other ways' (1995, p. 187).

NINE

Jumping ship – making your own way

In the previous chapter we used Fowler's staged theory of faith to provide a map for the faith journey. The use of the word 'journey' is significant, as a journey carries a number of important connotations. A journey, unlike a trip, is focused less on getting to a specific destination and more on the experience; the importance of being on the road. Like any long journey, the journey of faith involves times of preparation, times of difficult terrain, dead ends in which the path has to be retraced, detours, times of constant moving and times of rest and recuperation before the journey can be resumed. There are long-term resting points and other times when all that is possible is a brief nap on the road.

For many the decision to leave church is like choosing to leave a cruise ship on which they have been journeying. They are left clutching their cases on the wharf at a foreign port as they watch the liner steaming off to the next port without them. This can be a terribly lonely and scary experience. Yet it is a decision that for almost inexplicable reasons many know they have to make. But what can they do once they have left the ship? Is this the end of the journey? The end of the journey with God? Is this where Christian faith shrivels and finally dies?

For some, it would seem that a time spent navigating their own way and travelling light is part of what God is calling them to. To push the analogy further it appears that it is time to buy one's own small yacht and continue the journey; a journey which is substantially different from travelling on the liner and may involve a different course, new stopovers as well as new adventures, threats, dangers, excitements and opportunities. For those who remain on the liner, of course, it doesn't make any sense. Why get off when life on the cruise ship is so comfortable and safe? Yet for those who have experienced a major transition of faith there is often a deep realization that there can be no honest heartfelt enjoyment of travelling on the liner once the prospect of sailing your own yacht gets under your skin.

Having left the ship, leavers need some time to get their bearings, work through their grief, and plan the next phase of the journey. Taking time to work out where they are and finding their feet on dry land is the next step. But sooner or later, and preferably sooner, they need to get back on the water and move on again. The port they jumped ship at doesn't have to be the end of the journey. For many church leavers, space is needed to relive and work through the decision to leave the ship. Space to express their anger at what life on board the liner was doing to them. Space to articulate, if only to themselves, the pain, disappointment and maybe even abuse they felt on board.

Getting rid of the baggage of the liner is part of being ready to move on; you can't actually move on without taking the time to empty out everything that isn't necessary for the next leg on a much smaller craft. Dinner suits and make-up bags must now be traded for a compass, simple rations and waterproof clothing.

For some, the foreign port becomes a new home. The journey on the waves is forsaken. These include many of the Reflective Exiles of Chapter 5. While everyone who leaves the ship needs some time on shore to prepare for the next phase of the journey, many of the Reflective Exiles appear stuck on shore. In fact nearly 50 per cent of those I interviewed at the Reflective Exile stage had been there for five years or more and I got the feeling that many could be there for a long time to come, if not permanently.

For these port dwellers their energy is often expended emptying their baggage of stuff that reminds them of life on the liner. Many stayed on too long and left resentful of cruise ship culture. Their energy now is given to persuading others not to go on a cruise or to sharing their story in the local café or bar with others who have also left the cruise ships. Yet for most there remains a yearning for the sea, a desire to one day set off again. And maybe they will move on again, repack their bags, select another liner, yacht or fishing boat and move off the island. For the wind and the sea beckon them to the journey.

For some the temptation simply to get on the next liner that comes into port is very strong. Contemplating travelling the high seas in a little yacht can make the prospect of a warm bed on a safe liner appear awfully inviting. After months or even years in a foreign port we can understand the decision of those who do board the next passing liner rather than stay where they are indefinitely or take to the ocean in a smaller vessel. The idea of going it alone, or at best with a few other liner hoppers is frightening, and there are genuine and undeniable risks involved. Although joining the next cruise ship offers security and comfort, there remains something unnerving about standing on the deck and watching a passing yacht when we know we have turned down the opportunity to sail ourselves.

For most leavers the next phase of the journey requires a much smaller boat. It is inherently a personal journey; what would, in previous eras, have been called a pilgrimage. It is an inner journey more than it is an outer journey and therefore not one that is easily travelled on the liner. On the liner there are too many other passengers to rub up against. Too many organized activities. Too much external structure with meals at 8 a.m., noon and 6 p.m. and endless entertainment. This strict itinerary seems too restrictive now. And so the option of leasing a small yacht and going it alone or more often with a couple of others takes on a new passion while also providing a new fear.

For these leavers the smell of the sea and the thought of the wind on their face is too powerful to simply stay in port. They need to find their own way, to sail driven simply by the wind and feel the spray of the waves. So they find themselves down at the wharf sinking the last of their travellers' cheques into buying and outfitting a small yacht.

Before we look at their continued journey on the yacht, let's go back to understanding what it's like to jump ship.

Church isn't changing – I am!

Before jumping ship potential leavers begin to feel uneasy, dissatisfied and uncomfortable with much of ship life. People contemplating leaving church feel dissatisfied with their church life in a very similar way. This is a life they once found nurturing and encouraging. In fact the very aspects of church they used to get the most out of and for a long time wouldn't miss, now seem drab, uninviting and completely un-nurturing.

It's not that the church has changed – a point that often confuses both the potential leaver and those around them. The important change is what is going on within the individual.

People often try to reduce these feelings of dissatisfaction by changing either themselves or some aspect of the church so it better suits their perceived needs. Either they try to wake themselves up and find more enthusiasm and zeal for their faith or they try to change the church. Both inevitably fail to solve the problem. When you're tired of life on board the liner and no longer find it enjoyable, no end of pepping yourself up or trying to convince yourself that it is where you should be can change the underlying feelings of disgust, boredom and irrelevance. Yet, equally, trying to change some aspect of life on the cruise ship will not satisfy your growing need to sail your own vessel. You can change the menu, alter the daily on-board newspaper, rearrange the entertainment, even work to alter the itinerary but in the end you are still not sailing yourself. And ultimately you won't be satisfied until you do.

Although there may be aspects of your church that need to change, at this point in your own faith journey starting a campaign to bring about the changes will only drain you and leave the church leadership confused or actively working against your proposed changes. Now isn't the time for you to change the church. It is time for deep personal change. Even if you are successful in changing the worship or some other aspect of the church, in the long term it will not change the internal feeling of deep soul unease. In time similar feelings of unease will move to some other aspect of the church or the faith package of the church. Your time of helping to bring change within the life of a church may come later.

Too often church leaders suspect the way to keep dissatisfied people happy is to give them a role in the leadership or a significant leadership position within a specific aspect of the church. Particularly a role where they can be instrumental in bringing change in a way that they and perhaps the leadership feel is necessary. Potential leavers may well be correct in perceiving what needs to change but invariably this is not the time for them to bring it about.

What the leaver needs now is time, space, resources, understanding, validation and support for their own inner journey.

The most helpful thing anyone can give a person experiencing this phase of the Christian journey is to tell them it is normal. What they are experiencing doesn't mean that they are losing their faith. It doesn't mean that they are backsliding. What it does mean is that they are coming to a new refining and defining of their relationship with God, themselves and the world. The work that needs to be done at this point is internal work rather than trying to give energy to changing the structures of the Christian community to which they belong.

People seriously thinking about leaving the church need to know that for many Christians part of the faith journey is travelled in small yachts rather than big cruise ships. This means that getting off to go sailing is OK. That in leaving and setting out to sail in a smaller craft they are not mad or bad but simply following a well-worn path to maturity of faith. After all, even Jesus was led by the Spirit into the wilderness (Luke 4.1). This is the same Spirit that led Jesus to heal the sick, to speak with the crowd, argue with the Pharisees and that led him on the road that would end on a cross. In other words, the wilderness time too was part of God's leading.

If I simply can't leave

Despite the intensity of some people's feelings to the contrary, they realize that they cannot easily leave the cruise ship. Some work on the boat – their income, career, and family needs demand that they continue to do this. Others are employed in organizations connected with the cruise ship and it is a condition of their contract that they travel by liner. Still others have family reasons for staying. It might be OK for them personally to jump ship and go it alone but what about their children who may really enjoy it on board? Often parents see that it would be inappropriate to jump ship if it meant disrupting the emerging Christian faith of their children. What can we say to these people?

If you can't leave the ship, get some distance between yourself and those aspects of ship life that cause you the most distress. Forget the ship programme and life on the liner and focus on sailing. Hit the ship's library, find a deck chair in the remotest corner of the boat and get away from the crowd. Take a wander round the engine room or ask to see into the kitchens. Chat with the chefs, the engineers and the on-board repairmen.

Give some time for you and God. When the ship pulls into port go sailing instead of sightseeing. Hang around the jetty, talk with the sailboat owners, watch them cleaning, preparing and readying their yachts. Where possible go sailing. Sure you may not be able to jump ship, but could you join a yacht for a stage of the journey and meet the family and the liner at the next port?

What I am suggesting is that you distance yourself from the aspects of church life that irritate you and focus on what nurtures your faith. For some people doing some serious theological reading is helpful. For others it's taking a theological course or working towards a theological qualification. Some find that reading about or studying psychology, sociology, philosophy, world religions or history really grabs them. Many find pursuing their own inner spirituality helpful by going to a spiritual director, or attending seminars, liturgical services and retreats. Others find learning to listen to and trust their own emotions, feelings and intuitions brings significant growth.

At this point of the journey, gaining an increased self-understanding and knowledge is important. The Myers-Briggs personality type indicator, the Enneagram[1] and other self-knowledge tools can be helpful. Counselling and spiritual direction are often important components of this part of the journey.

So at this stage, it is important to give time and energy to this twofold movement: the move away from those things that had previously nurtured your faith that are now increasingly barren and repulsive to you, and the move towards doing the things that you find nurture your faith now. Cut yourself some slack! In doing so you will have some time to invest in other areas. These two suggestions need to go hand in hand. Reducing your involvement in areas that frustrate you without taking the saved time and energy and using it in faith-building ways is not a way forward.

While in Australia, as part of my research I met with a leader in one church where they had a practice for supporting potential church leavers. Whenever the church leadership thought that a church member could be beginning to move away or was seriously struggling in their Christian faith they would arrange for a pastorally astute church member to meet with them and talk through how they were feeling. If they found the person was actually struggling with their faith and continued church involvement they would then make two suggestions.

First, they told the person that they should feel free to come or not come to church or any church activity as they wished. The church would not remove them from the church roll, or speak badly of them. The church leadership would continue to inform them about and invite them to church activities and they would be welcome at any they chose to attend. In this way the church leadership gave them the personal space that they would need.

Second, they would ask that the person use the time they would have spent involved in church in other ways that nurtured their faith. For example, people were encouraged to see a spiritual director or a counsellor, to do a theological course, visit a city mission where people work with the poor and marginalized, begin new ways of prayer, start writing a journal, even attend services at other churches. Finally they would offer the person the opportunity to meet occasionally with anyone in the church leadership they felt they could connect with, to encourage them and support them in this phase of their faith journey.

What impressed me about the attitude of this church was its primary focus on the individual and their Christian faith. The church's priority was not to keep them coming to their church or even any other church. The focus was on helping them to find ways to nurture their own development and maturing of Christian faith. To help this happen they were prepared to give them the freedom to attend other groups and connect with others, knowing that they might later move away.

The real gain for the church in taking this initiative is that should the person decide to leave, they leave without increased animosity towards the church and they know the focus of the church leadership is on their best interests and the continued growth of their Christian faith. Should they later consider returning to a church, no hurdle has been built in the process of leaving that would distract them. Sadly, far too often people leave EPC churches with the feeling, correct or otherwise, that *they* were not important and all that really mattered to the church leadership was what they could give to the church.

Another important gift someone can give the struggler is to connect them with an experienced and empathetic companion. This is someone who has travelled their own inner journey, who knows the dislocation of their own faith package unravelling around them. Someone who knows the importance of giving them space, and the room to say what they feel (no matter how seemingly negative, blunt, or faith-destroying it may be). The companion needs to be someone who has journeyed with God beyond their own time of wilderness and deep faith darkness. They need to be a companion who brings hope that faith can live again. Of course, the companion's faith journey may be quite different from that of the person they are companioning. A friend of mine found a real sense of connection in reformed theology; others have made new connections with creation spirituality, gardening or feminist spirituality. None of these avenues have been part of my own story but the friends who have taken them have been highly supportive of my own wanderings, meanderings and eventual sources of nurture.

The companion needs to be someone who is not scared of others dismantling their EPC faith. Someone who is not out to defend the faith or God. Someone who realizes that God is big enough to cope with genuine struggle and disappointment and they need to be that way too. Someone who is secure in their own faith and therefore not rocked by others deconstructing theirs. Someone who is not going to get squeamish if you rant and rave, yell and scream or dismiss their own beliefs. Having said this, it is equally important that the companion be able to tell their own faith story with conviction and quietly speak of the core elements of their own faith. When you're feeling shipwrecked yourself, it is the outstretched hand of someone who has a firm grip of the lifebuoy you need, rather than the outstretched hand of a drowning person who may well take you both down.

The companion needs to be someone you connect with easily. Someone you can trust, and someone for whom there is a positive personal chemistry. They need to be available to spend the time with you that you need. To revisit the analogy of sailing, it is like choosing an experienced sailor to maintain radio contact with as you sail your new yacht to the next port. You need to have an inherent and deep trust in their ability and a strong sense that if you get into trouble their advice and experience is worth having.

ACCEPTING THE LOSSES

Leaving the cruise ship means real losses, particularly the companionship of fellow travellers. Giving up church, even when you are dissatisfied with it, brings its own losses. Perhaps most significant is the loss of a community of people to be a part of. Many of the church leavers I have spoken to have been surprised by the intensity of this loss. No longer is there a gathered community of people to join each Sunday morning. There are no 'hellos' from people they've known for years or even smiles from those they vaguely know. There's no newsletter and no sense of being part of a community with its gossip and politicking, news of people unwell, babies born and new romances. This is a real loss.

Coupled with the loss of the sense of a wider community there is often the loss of deeper friendships. People who have left believing their friendships would survive are often surprised just how few of those seemingly close relationships actually do. I have spoken to far too many who are bewildered by how few of their church friends even make contact after they have left. Often these are people they have worked with on church committees, activities and groups for years. They have been in and out of each other's homes and felt they had a genuine friendship. It is even worse when, months later, they meet in a mall or supermarket and realize they simply have nothing in common any more and it is painfully obvious their old friends feel uncomfortable about bumping into them.

A COMPASS FOR SAILING

When it comes to preparing for a journey on a small yacht a compass is an essential requirement. Of course, a compass isn't normally essential for the cruise ship traveller, but once alone it becomes really important. A compass points ahead of your present position and indicates the direction you need to move in order to reach the goal. Assuming the goal is continued and deepening faith in God, it can be helpful to look at the lives of previous journeyers who recorded their own travels through difficult times. Looking at the Old Testament journey of Job can often be helpful as a rough guide of what lies ahead.

In the opening verses of the book of Job we meet a man who has been blessed by God and has a firm foundation of faith. A man with a scrupulous concern for sin and a fear that either he or one of his children could fail God. He is someone who both God and Satan could agree was very good. Job is a man who sees the presence of God in the good things that he has been given and acknowledges them as blessings from God. Yet despite Job's faith, thankfulness to God and scrupulous focus on remaining sinless he is, nevertheless, taken through a horrendous unpicking of his faith. In effect, he hits the wall. The wall is the place where faith is dislocated. Job is thrown into a new and confusing world. The old trust in the beliefs of the faith of the time are now replaced with unanswered questions and deep doubts.

Although his friends remind him of the orthodox teachings of the community of faith he cannot accept them. They simply do not connect with his new experience of life. He can no longer accept that sickness and suffering is the result of sin. Rather his confidence in the beliefs and teaching of the community of faith has been usurped by his own internal authority, which tells him their recipe doesn't work. Throughout the book there is an increasing self-confidence, which gives Job the courage to disagree with his friends and rail against God. Where before God was shown to Job through blessings and external criteria, it is now only the absence and silence of God that remain for him. A life previously built on the beliefs and teaching of faith is now overwhelmed by the pain and reality of his experience, which speaks with new truth and disqualifies the answers of the past. This is the second phase of Job's journey, a phase dominated by doubt and questions, by anger and disappointment with God. Job's confidence in his lived experience is now much stronger than past convictions and the recipes of faith offered by others. It is a time of critically unpacking his faith and an angry search for the God who seems to have disappeared.

Yet Job is not left there, because there is a final stage to the book of Job, the place in which Job comes to a bigger meeting with God. It is the place that Hagberg and Guelich call 'the wall'. This is a place that many encounter somewhere between the transition from a stage three faith as outlined by Fowler and before settling into the stage five expression of faith. The wall is a place where a new layer of transformation occurs. Hagberg and Guelich define it by saying: 'The wall represents our will meeting God's will face-to-face. We decide anew whether we are willing to surrender and let God direct our lives' (Hagberg and Guelich, 1989, p. 114).

135

Facing the wall is a significant encounter; nothing compares with the intensity and struggle of the journey through the wall. It is what St John of the Cross called 'the dark night of the soul'. Though we try, often desperately, we cannot simply scale it, circumvent it, burrow under it, leap over it or ignore it. The wall remains and commands our attention as the boils, sickness and destitute state of Job demanded his undivided attention.

Although we are invariably unaware of it, the wall is holy ground and passing through it brings as rich an encounter of God as life offers. Yet paradoxically it is at the same time frightening and unpredictable. It is a place of deep encounter with God and of deep spiritual and psychological healing. As Hagberg and Guelich say:

> Mystery lies at the core of the wall, a mystery that ultimately defies explanation but includes discomfort, surrender, healing, awareness, forgiveness, acceptance, love, closeness to God, discernment, melting, moulding, and solitude and reflection. (Hagberg and Guelich, 1989, p. 120)

The journey through the wall has four phases: awareness, forgiveness, acceptance and love. It begins with an increased 'awareness of our shadow sides and hidden parts . . . It means being aware of all the lies we have accepted about ourselves and our families and all the myths of life that were never true' (Hagberg and Guelich, 1989, p. 121). It means finding out who we are as opposed to who we would like to be or others want us to be. This new awareness is often accompanied with feelings of anger, bitterness and sadness.

The second phase involves a deep forgiving of ourselves and others. It means forgiving in new ways both ourselves and those who have hurt us. It involves a new encounter with the grace and forgiveness of God. This awareness and forgiveness can be accompanied by a new acceptance, an acceptance that goes a step further than forgiveness. It is a new embracing and compassionate holding of the deep currents of our lives, an embracing and holding of our own humanness, failure and sexuality. It is an acceptance that

> means looking at ourselves in a detached way and celebrating the full range of our humanness. It means embracing the clown, the devil, the frightened child, the wicked witch, the lonely lover, the intellectual snob, the over-

achiever, the arrogant elitist, the insecure boy or girl, the outlandish dresser, the attention-seeker, the fool, the risk-taker, the addicted one, the beauty queen, or the perfectionist. (Hagberg and Guelich, 1989, p. 122)

The last phase of the wall involves a new emergence of love. Love for God, ourselves and others. 'This love, rooted in awareness, forgiveness and acceptance of ourselves, differs profoundly from what we have known before' (Hagberg and Guelich, 1989, p. 122). It is a love rooted in self-knowledge and the knowledge of the encounter of God with us that realizes that evil and sin lie in us all and yet we can be loved. Such knowledge is far deeper than a head or intellectual understanding; rather it is a knowledge founded on a deep inner transformation. Because of this transformation the journeyer is increasingly able to love others.

This is the experience of Job. When he has spent his anger and questions on God he is surprisingly encountered by God in a new way. God gives him a new perspective. He is taken to see the creation, the making of the universe, the animals of the deep and this changes his perspective of himself, of God and of his suffering. He is not given an answer to his questions, the riddle of suffering is not solved, nor even addressed. But as the French philosopher Paul Ricoeur states:

> The God who addresses Job out of the tempest shows him Behemoth and Leviathan, the hippopotamus and the crocodile, vestiges of the chaos that has been overcome, representing a brutality dominated and overcome by the creative act. Through these symbols he gives him to understand that all is order, measure and beauty – inscrutable order, measure beyond measure, terrible beauty. (Ricoeur, 1967, p. 321)

This new encounter with God changes Job's perspective as he experiences a universe of 'inscrutable order, measure beyond measure and terrible beauty'. The realm of the mysteries of God is entered. It is as though God is speaking a new language to Job now and the old seems simplistic babbling in the wake of the new. His relationship with God changes: 'My ears had heard of you but now my eyes have seen you', he says (Job 42.5). Job's journey through the wall has brought a new encounter with God, a face-to-face encounter, which is life- and faith-defining. Job is humbled by this experience, left only to put his hand over his mouth

(Job 40.4), for God is much bigger than he had previously appreciated. With this humbling comes a softening within him.

This is a major shift for Job. Now instead of arguing with his companions who have spent chapters trying to tell him his sickness and destitution is all his own fault, Job chooses to pray for them. He doesn't try to rub his friends' noses in their wrong or remind them of their aggressiveness towards him, but is free to pray for them and care for them.

His softening and new inclusiveness is also hinted at in the final section of the book, where only the names of his daughters are mentioned and to whom, with his sons, he gives an inheritance. He gives this to his daughters despite the Old Testament teaching of Numbers 27 where only sons were entitled to receive an inheritance.

This is a move to a new understanding and experience of God, an experience beyond the wall. An experience Ricoeur calls a 'second or willed naïveté'. It is a new phase, which involves both of Job's experiences of God brought together to form a new whole. The time of knowing the external God through doctrines and recipes of faith, external blessings and faithful obedience coupled with the time of despair, darkness, wilderness and the absence of God in which all is silent and faith is dry and tasteless. Ricoeur uses the image of a knot made from two strands of rope to symbolize these two previous states of faith, which are tied together to form a much deeper new phase. This is a phase rich in the mysteries and presence of God, where teaching, Scripture and doctrine give, and the reality of life interprets.

It is the place the American jurist Oliver Wendell Holmes summed up by saying:

> For simplicity on this side of complexity,
> I would not give you a fig,
> But for simplicity on the other side of complexity,
> for that I would give you anything I have. (Quoted in Fowler, 1996, p. 177)

This is the goal of faith for those who find their previous faith dislocating and shattering within them. It is not the journey away from pain, doubt and confusion but the journey through struggle to a new appreciation of God at work. At times I have used the following very simple analogy to explain this. The first phase, faith prior to the wall, can be likened to the shell of the crab. Here faith, beliefs, doctrine and ethics form a shell around the person. A shell which protects them from the outside world and which is the first thing others encounter. The second phase can be likened to the vulnerable crab when it loses its shell. Here the crab is stripped of its protection from the world and looks soft, even pathetic to those who observe it. Of course, the crab is very vulnerable between shells; yet to grow to maturity the old shell must be shed and time given for the new to form.

To explain the final stage we must move away from the crab and imagine a species with an endoskeleton such as mammals. Not an external shell but an internal skeleton which replaces the need for the old external shell. A skeleton which provides a spine of belief and faith and yet is covered by flesh and is soft to the touch. This is the Job of the final chapter of the book who is deeply aware of the reality of God, of God's order, measure and beauty in all things and is at the same time soft, humble and open to the needs of others.

We can liken the story of Job to a compass because it offers hope for the dark journey; despite the darkness, the pain and the loneliness of Job's journey God does come to him. It is hopeful because although Job experiences the complete dislocation of the doctrines and externally focused faith of his past, there is the building of a new and unspeakable faith. By the end of the book, Job has learnt to combine the faith of old and his experience of life in all its pain and struggle together with a new glimpse of the wonders of God. The old is not lost and nor is the pain of the journey lost, but they are reconfigured on a much larger canvas – a canvas formed from a new perspective of God.

To journey through the wall we must experience something of the despair of faith that Job felt; the complete dislocation of our faith and the sense that we are being forced through the mincer. Yet the journey through the wall leads to tremendous gains. A softening of our personality and faith, which incorporates a greater acceptance of our own humanity and allows us to accept the humanity of others. A new acceptance of others that can look past their behaviour and shadow sides and accept them with all the insecurities, fears and ambitions that motivate them.

Beyond the wall is a place of deep forgiveness. The wall itself is often a place of lament and is truly our own wailing wall. It is where old hurts, deep anxieties, past shames and personal wounds are connected with the pain of God, and where some experience the mingling of their tears with the tears of God. It is a place where the incarnate God – the 'God with us' – can be a special source of illumination. A place where the teachings and experience of Jesus recorded in the Gospels can be filled with meaning and new intrigue.

The move beyond the wall typically involves a new openness and depth of connection with others, a new energy for giving and forgiving. There is a new desire to connect with others who are different from ourselves. It is a phase that connects with what Erikson called the Generative phase of life – a stage where encouraging and endorsing the growth of others takes on a special satisfaction. People often experience a new desire to connect with mission endeavours and give themselves, without losing themselves, to the needs of others. Contributing to the wider community in ways shaped and motivated by their faith is both an outworking of the journey through the wall and for many an important practical part of the journey through the wall. Even when we hit the wall there is much that we have to give and need to continue to give to others.

It may appear that I have romanticized, even idealized this journey. This was not my intent. But I do intend to point, as a compass does, to true north – to the best of outcomes from the journey of dislocation. To point to the hope of deep faith, a fulfilled life and rich experiences of God, ourselves and others. I do intend to point beyond the wall, to sketch the new stage of Christian faith which can open up for people after the demoralizing, painful and confusing journey through the wall. To say that, though it doesn't seem as though it could ever be possible in the despair of the journey through the wall, the wall does come to an end. Eventually when we have painfully taken down the last brick a new vista of God at work can unfold before us.

NOTE

1 The Enneagram is a self-awareness tool that focuses on people's uncon-scious motivations. Many people find this a very informative tool for gaining increasing self-awareness, especially in terms of their spirituality.

TEN

Leaver-sensitive churches

Leavers need you

Often EPC church leaderships are confused, even threatened, by people's decisions to leave. This is especially true when the leavers are not planning to join another church. As some people are leaving the church those in leadership are often also aware of new people choosing to join the church, make commitments of faith or commenting very positively about church life, worship and teaching. These mixed messages from those leaving through the 'back door' and those coming in the 'front door' are often difficult to unravel. All too often those in church leadership find it more convenient to let existing members slip away while they focus their attention on those coming in the front door. But there are good reasons for church leaderships to look more carefully at their back-door leavers.

We are aware of the biblical connection of good leaders and a shepherd. The analogy seeps through Scripture in a number of places, but perhaps none more clearly than in Ezekiel 34, where it is written of the leaders of the people that:

> You have not strengthened the weak or healed the sick or bound up the injured. You have not brought back the strays or searched for the lost . . . For this is what the Sovereign Lord says: I myself will search for my sheep and look after them. As a shepherd looks after his scattered flock when he is with them, so I will look after my sheep. I will rescue them from all the places where they were scattered on a day of clouds and darkness . . . I will bring them into their own land . . . I will tend them in a good pasture, and the mountain heights of Israel will be their grazing land. (Ezekiel 34.4, 11–14)

Jesus also spoke of the distinction between shepherds and hired hands, the crucial difference being the way a good shepherd would leave the 99 sheep in search of the one who had wandered off. Today in our context it would seem too few EPC church leaders take this passage seriously. Like the hired hands, it would appear that they are happier sitting with the flock than doing the hard work, maybe even personally risky work, of scouring the heights and ledges for those that have wandered off. We need to remember that in Matthew's Gospel the story of the lost sheep ends with the words, 'In the same way your Father in heaven is not willing that any of these little ones should be lost' (Matthew 18.14).

In order to support the continued Christian faith of potential and past church leavers we need churches willing to invest personal and corporate energy into being good shepherds. Yet today too often the model of a successful pastor in the EPC church scene is the visionary leader more at home with the language and techniques of corporate management than the concerns of shepherds. The ancient crook carried by bishops as a reminder to themselves and the church of their calling is now more often replaced with the techniques of a 1980s chief executive officer (CEO)[1] complete with growth-focused management and marketing tools.

Your church needs the leavers

During one evening at Spirited Exchanges recently, someone involved in the business environment made the comment that they couldn't understand why churches would simply let people leave without finding out why they became dissatisfied and then doing something about it. He finished by saying, 'That would never happen in the corporate world because that information is like gold.' Yet in our EPC churches we seem to expend huge amounts of energy, expense and prayer to bring people into the churches through the front door while ignoring the seepage of previously committed people out the back door.

While any leakage is significant and worthy of the leaders' attention, the loss of the kind of people I met during the course of my research doesn't make sense. Many of those I have met have formed the core leadership of their church and were among the most creative, thoughtful and committed of the church leaders. These are the people who the church depended on in previous years to lead their worship, run their home groups and care for the children and teenagers. People who had a creative and thoughtful edge to their faith and often encouraged others in their commitment. Our churches can ill afford to lose such people. It seems the words of the prophet Haggai ring with new clarity: 'Your wages are stored in bags full of holes' (Haggai 1.6, CEV). Our churches cannot continue to develop as genuine communities of faith while we let people drop out without seeking to address their concerns and needs. It is not helpful for them or the ongoing life of the church.

Over recent years I have observed, with a growing sense of anxiety, how groups of highly committed people have asked their church leadership for some place within the church to process the typical issues and concerns of potential church leavers. Too often church leaders either ignore their request or force them to choose between staying in the church or forming a group to explore their questions and concerns. Eventually many just leave. Watching this process has led me to believe that this is the most unhelpful platform for the individual's continued journey of faith and disposition to the church.

Leavers take their time, skills, efforts and wallets with them

The leavers I've met were predominantly in their thirties and forties when they left their churches. At this stage of life many are heading into their most productive years in their respective careers and businesses. Now, when they are nearing the height of their earning capacity, have developed a well-honed skill set and have some maturity of faith, they leave. As they leave, all the resources they have to give to the life of the church and mission go with them.

One of the cries heard from church leaders is a concern about the lack of mature Christians to lead mission and church ministry ventures. Sadly, many of the people the EPC church has helped to bring to faith, discipled and trained up have now slipped out the back door. The very people who could have helped fill the leadership roles we so desperately need to fill. This is an obvious point to make but it comes with an added sting. Imagine what a church leadership could be like if some of the leavers who negotiated their own faith dislocation, the darkness of the wall experience and the experience of God reforming their faith, were part of our church leadership. Imagine the depths of commitment, maturity and trust in God these people would bring to our churches. Losing people like this is nothing short of a tragedy for the church.

Even on a purely financial basis the loss of such people is a significant area of concern. Many now at the height of their giving potential simply walk out the back door. Even a profit-driven CEO of the 1980s ilk can see the futility of this. Yet most of the leavers I met said that when they left no one from the church leadership came to talk with them or seemed to care about why they were leaving. By their silence the church leadership reinforced their decision to leave.

Leavers tell their stories to others

Inevitably leavers tell their stories and experiences of the EPC church to their friends, workmates and family members. The stories I've heard from such leavers would surely act as powerful disincentives to Christian faith, and EPC churches in particular, for anyone who hears them. Particularly when friends, family members and workmates have seen the person so involved and committed to church now walking away with horror stories. Surely this cannot be a good advertisement for EPC churches or the Christian faith?

Even where putting time and effort into leavers does not lead to them coming back to the church, it can significantly reduce the negativity of their experiences and their stories – the stories they will inevitably tell those who are close to them.

Leavers take their children with them

The children of leavers almost always leave church as well. In the process it would appear that many of these children are inoculated against the Christian church and quite possibly the Christian faith for a very long time to come. Having experienced something of church life and then watched their parents leave, the prospect of these children choosing to come back later seems extremely small.

While their parents have often developed a rich store of Christian knowledge and experience, from which they can draw while outside the church, their children often have very little to draw on. The parents may be entering a deeply internal stage of their Christian faith while many of their children are at the point where they need a peer group, clear boundaries and sharper definitions and understandings of what it means to be a follower of Jesus Christ. The parents may need leaders who will allow them space to chew over the grey and difficult issues of their own faith, while their children need leaders who can act as strong role models and encouragers.

While the Christian faith, and church involvement in particular, have been in steady decline, recent studies suggest that at best EPC churches are barely maintaining stable numbers of attenders. In this context church leaderships can no longer afford to be blasé about the people they lose. Working hard to bring new people into the church while letting longer-term, highly committed people slip out the back door achieves little. It is time EPC church leaderships woke up and realized something needs to be done and that they have a significant role to play.

Leaver-sensitive churches

In the 1990s some EPC churches became 'seeker sensitive'. In many such churches the services, preaching and church activities were tailored for those interested in the Christian faith. While this has been a very positive step in church life we also need to become 'leaver sensitive'. Not only do church leaderships need to give energy, time and prayer to the needs of seekers but we also need to give the same energy, time and prayer to leavers. Being leaver sensitive is not difficult to achieve and may prove to be as significant for the long-term health and viability of EPC churches as the effort put into being seeker sensitive. In fact the two can work hand in hand ensuring a holistic perspective within the church and a greater point of connection with the wider society.

A leaver-sensitive church is one that is aware of and seeks to address the concerns of leavers and potential leavers. Discussions with leavers and what we have learned at Spirited Exchanges lead me to suggest that a leaver-sensitive church would incorporate some of the following characteristics.

PROVIDE PLACES FOR PEOPLE TO EXPLORE, QUESTION
AND TO DOUBT

Too often the understanding of Christian faith in EPC churches precludes exploration, questioning and doubt. Yet each has a place within the matrix of Christian faith. In fact, faith is built on the tension between doubt and trust, suspicion and certitude. Doubt is no more the enemy of Christian faith than certitude is. Yet where are the places in EPC churches where people can express serious doubts and questions about their Christian faith? Where in your church is there room for people to say, 'Prayer doesn't work', 'God has left me', 'I don't know that I believe in salvation, evangelism, hell, creation (or any other major area of faith)'? We need to realize that God is in the question as well as the answer and that living with the questions is part of the journey.

The creation of a safe space in which difficult things can be said, brought out into the open and explored, is an important environment for many people's journeys of faith and understanding of God at work in their lives. This is a place where doubts can be listened to and allowed to be, without anyone trying to change the person's mind or put them right. Certainly without anyone quoting a Bible verse to them.

This is the kind of environment we seek to create each time Spirited Exchanges meets; a place where people are free to express their viewpoint, understanding and experience on a particular aspect of faith in a free-floating and non-judgemental conversation. Spirited Exchanges gives people a safe space, space to think, to reflect, space to give voice to their doubts and fears, their questions and sense of unbelief. Space to berate and be angry with what isn't working for them. Space to grieve for dreams and a way of faith lost. It gives them space to create some distance between themselves and much of church life, while still being connected to a community of faith and people who are sensitive and empathetic to their journey.

Where churches consider starting such a group, careful selection of people involved and of the nature of the group activity is needed.

PROVIDE A THEOLOGY OF JOURNEY

Often preaching and teaching in EPC churches can emphasize coming to Christian faith and then say little about the rest of the journey. Yet the

Scriptures teach that we were brought into being out of the abundance of God's love and called to be transformed into union with God. This is an ongoing and demanding journey. There are lots of names for this journey of transformation: spiritual regeneration, deification, divinization, Christification, transformation in Christ, spiritualization, interiorization, sanctification. Whatever we call it, there is a process, a journey through which 'we shall become mature people, reaching to the very height of Christ's full stature' (Ephesians 4.13, GNB).

For many people it would help if this journey were talked about, preached about and discussed in the life of the church. If the spiritual high points and low points of biblical characters were spoken of and their journeys unfolded for people. If the great classics of the Christian journey, like St John of the Cross, St Teresa of Avila, were mentioned and explained. While resources that make sense of the journey of faith can be drawn from Scripture and the classical writers, there are also other sources. For example, novels about the Christian journey like *Pilgrim's Progress, Hinds' Feet on High Places*,[2] or theories outlining the stages of faith as those used by James Fowler, M. Scott Peck and many others. These resources need to be part of church teaching and seminars.

As part of developing these resources of the journey it is important to speak openly about the dark places of the Christian faith, the absence of God and the times when God hides his face from people. It would have helped many of the leavers I have spoken with if, in the midst of difficult phases of their own journey, they were able to share their story in the life of the church alongside those who have experienced some victory or real success. By doing these things churches prepare and resource people for the difficult and confusing parts of their own spiritual journey. In effect they are telling them that these times are normal and parts of many people's Christian experience. They are reinforcing the hope that the God who can seem so absent at times, reappears later with more clarity and connection than people may have experienced before. Encouraging people to talk about the difficulties and struggles of their Christian journey, even when there is no happy ending, lets people see the wall experience in other's lives and what they gain from it.

PROVIDE RESOURCES FOR PEOPLE IN THE DARK PLACES

Leavers have often commented to me that it would have helped them if churches taught people that feeling your faith is falling apart and losing relevance may not mean you are 'backsliding' or inevitably losing your faith. Rather for many people these experiences are simply part of the journey. Coupled with this they have said it would have helped if people were encouraged to move away from those aspects of church that used to be enormously helpful to them in the past, but which now irritate them. Not simply to move away though, but to replace those times with things that nurture their ongoing faith. For many the resources of spiritual direction, counselling, prayer journalling and theological study could be talked about and encouraged.

People do need to be reminded of the struggles of faith of others and also encouraged to take responsibility for their own faith. This means learning to lean into the difficult times and hang on to God even when there seems to be no answer and the heavens are barred. There is a tendency in us all to put faith down when it gets really tough and confusing, to simply shelve it or place the blame on the church. Yet at these times energy and determination are needed to look for the new things that God is raising up and find the new language in which God is speaking. A significant part of this energy and motivation can come from a caring community.

PROVIDE MODELS OF OTHER THEOLOGICAL UNDERSTANDINGS

For many leavers the only theology they know is a fairly conservative evangelicalism. While this is a valid expression of biblical theology, there are other perspectives that many find insightful and useful in rounding out and developing their faith during transition and crisis points. After all, God is much bigger than any single theological perspective. For some leavers, an understanding of the strengths of liberation theology, feminist theologies and black theologies is enormously helpful. Some find a recognition of biblical criticism and exegetical methods helpful. In fact, many feel deceived when they find through their own exploration a knowledge of biblical criticism, and realize that their pastors understood, but never mentioned, these issues to their congregation.

PROVIDE MODELS OF AN HONEST CHRISTIAN LIFE RATHER THAN 'SHOULDS'

Leavers say they needed to begin with where they actually were in their Christian faith. It would have helped them if an honest recognition and acceptance of people's present Christian faith had been encouraged and spoken of. Nearly a hundred years ago Bishop J. C. Ryle said he had come to the conclusion that 'the vast majority of professing Christians did not pray at all' (quoted in Houston, 1989, p. 16). I am sure that little has changed since. Certainly many people in their thirties and forties who have been Christians for years have told me they don't pray. They rarely connect with the worship time in church and often find the sermon completely irrelevant to their daily lives. Yet they go along each week for years and years accepting the constant diet of 'shoulds' that bear little relation to their own spiritual life. Creating an environment where these realities can be talked about honestly and unashamedly can be a very important motivation for change. By accepting the reality of their faith life they are then free to consider how they want to move on.

PROVIDE ROOM FOR EMOTIONS AND INTUITIONS

In some EPC circles there is a distrust of emotions and intuitions in favour of particular biblical interpretations of what a Christian 'should' feel. This can set up a dishonesty between what people think is acceptable and the reality of their own feelings and intuitions. As part of going through what Fowler calls 'the stage three to four transition' and the experience of the wall, many gain a new appreciation of the strength and validity of their emotions and intuitions and the way God speaks through them. Often such avenues are the new language, the unexplored language through which they experience God speaking to them. Yet years of being told feelings and intuitions are unreliable, of the flesh, even of the devil, can seriously erode either their new trust in God speaking through these aspects of their selfhood or their old trust of the teaching of the church. Either way it is unhelpful for people struggling with Christian faith.

To model this, churches need to include in their worshipping life space for the corporate lament and the cry of the psalmist and others, of 'Where are you, God?'

Finally, church leaders need to understand the leaving process and be able to pick the early and relatively obvious clues that people are going through a faith struggle. What are the clues?

- A slow and growing dissatisfaction in people who were otherwise settled and very happy with church life.
- Dissatisfaction in aspects of the church that people were previously very happy about, yet now no longer seem to connect with, e.g. the worship.
- Withdrawal from church activities outside of the main service, including leadership roles and home groups, without any attempt to replace these commitments with new areas.
- Changing patterns of church attendance and involvement. Some people come to church fortnightly, others weekly and some monthly or even less frequently. Pastors need to note people's normal pattern of attendance and take note when such a pattern changes. It may indicate something is changing for the person.
- A change in seating patterns may also be indicative of something deeper going on. People tend to sit in roughly similar places at church services. When this changes consistently over a period of time it may indicate some change of attitude. This is particularly the case when front row people become back row people.
- Tentative raising of a faith struggle, doubt or alternative theological viewpoint by someone who has previously been quite content in their understanding of Christian faith.
- People offering to lead the children's programme or work in the crèche. Although there are many reasons people offer to help lead the children's programme, I was surprised how many leavers said this was an acceptable transition point for them in their process of leaving the church.

When leaders become aware of clues that may indicate someone is struggling with their faith or their church involvement, the best strategy is to go and listen to them and ask if their observations are indicating anything. Leavers are far more open to discussion than church leaders might expect.

NOTES

1 The CEO model often espoused by church leaders appears to have more in common with the authoritarian, profit-driven corporate leadership style of the 1980s than that of corporate CEOs I meet with today.

2 *Hinds' Feet on High Places*: An allegory dramatizing the journey each of us must take before we can live in 'high places', by Hannah Hurnard.

ELEVEN

Searching for a place to belong

They drew a circle that shut me out
Heretic, rebel, a thing to flout
But love and I had the wit to win
We drew a circle that took them in.

Edwin Markham[1]

In the process of distancing themselves from their church and its EPC faith package, Stuart and Michelle met up with two other couples who were thinking and feeling similarly about their EPC church. Their common experience drew them together and they began meeting on a regular basis to discuss the source of their dissatisfactions and what they could do to try and overcome them. These discussions led them to form a group which met for nearly five years. Once underway the group quickly grew with anywhere between 12 and 20 people attending each week.

> *Michelle* We thought, 'What could we do, how could we do church differently?' Having spent a year talking, we got to the point where we actually felt we had to put feet to our ideas. For me it just kind of evolved, it grew and I suddenly found I wanted to do something about my life and make a choice, and my choice was that I didn't want to be where I was. I couldn't see anywhere else that I wanted to be anymore.

When the group had been going for three years Michelle described the experience, saying it had been an oasis for them.

> *Michelle* These three years have been an oasis. I feel as if I have moved into a level of intimacy with people which I had previously only touched with particular individuals in my life but never as part of a corporate group. I feel I share things which are very costly for me to share, which make me very vulnerable and I feel that I am known all the more deeply for it. I really feel accepted and I feel I can ask my really tough questions, even though I seldom get answers, as they are a group who don't give pat answers.

I really find it a very affirming place to be and I don't feel now that I am split, that I am here six days a week and expected to be someone else on Sundays. Now some of that may be my own interpretation of what I was expected to be. I am not saying that the church necessarily did that to me, but that was how I perceived it.

Describing his initial hopes for the group, Stuart talked of a place that had a high priority for openness and honesty, that would make Christianity relevant to people's daily lives and their work situations. A group that had an informally structured interactive environment and was a place of theological depth. For Stuart it needed to be somewhere that allowed for educated people who had left Pentecostal and charismatic churches, who didn't want to go back to traditional churches.

For many EPC church leavers, groups such as the one Stuart and Michelle began are an important part of their continued journey of faith outside the church. Such groups support and help shape their future faith. Naturally, the way these groups function varies greatly. Some are gatherings of those considering leaving a church; others are discussion groups primarily focused on the concerns of Reflective Exiles; while others are attempts to be 'church' in a new way for those who have left their church. The majority of church leavers I have met either are or want to be part of such post-church groups. These groups are called 'post-church' because they are groups formed by people who are themselves 'post-church' (people who have left or are only marginally involved in the institutional forms of church). The title also indicates that these groups are not connected to any institutional form of the church or church structures. They are called post-church with a hyphen because the hyphen draws attention to the fact that the groups are provisional; they are groups that are evolving and developing as they seek to be qualitatively different from the EPC churches they have left.[2]

Of those I formally interviewed, 65 per cent talked of being part of a group either in the process of leaving their church or after leaving. A further 9 per cent of the leavers were part of informal networks of people who had also left EPC churches. Only a minority of leavers (26 per cent) had not been involved in regularly meeting groups or informal networks of fellow leavers.

Not surprisingly, being a part of one or more of these post-church

Table 11.1 Proportion of leavers who belong to non-church groups

Faith positions	Involved in groups	
	No.	**%**
Disillusioned Followers (19)	8	42
Reflective Exiles (32)	15	47
Transitional Explorers (26)	21	81
Integrated Wayfinders (30)	26	87
Totals (107)	**70**	**65**

groups has a significant influence on them. They help to provide a sense of connection for many leavers. The influence of these groups on people's faith positions is shown in Table 11.1.

Fifty per cent of the Disillusioned Followers and Reflective Exiles interviewed were not part of post-church groups or informal networks compared with only 3.5 per cent of the Transitional Explorers and Integrated Wayfinders. These figures could be explained two ways. Either the decision to be part of a group and the influence of the group has a significant impact on church leavers' subsequent development of faith, or Transitional Explorers and Integrated Wayfinders are more likely to want to associate with others of like faith in small groups. Having thought about this relationship for some time and spoken with many leavers I believe both explanations are involved. Choosing to be part of a group does help nurture and support further faith development, but it is equally true that the Transitional Explorers and Integrated Wayfinders typically desire to associate with others of like faith.

It appears that those who do *not* meet with others in the process of leaving or after leaving are less likely to move on from their faith position at the time of leaving the church. This indicates that we should not underestimate the importance of fellow travellers on the faith journey. In all difficult journeys, including the difficult phases of the Christian faith, companionship is an enormous strength, motivation and reassurance. Melanie, for example, describes the importance of the group she belongs to:

Melanie When we started our group we were all feeling these tensions, but we really didn't want to lose, we didn't feel that it was helpful to struggle as individuals with these things. We realized there was a bigger pattern, not just what we were feeling as individuals.

There also seems to be a strong relationship between group involvement during the process of leaving and a person's faith position. The Transitional Explorers and Integrated Wayfinders were more likely to have joined a group in the process of leaving than the Disillusioned Followers and Reflective Exiles.

For nine of the interviewees there had been no formal non-church-based group affiliation but an informal network had provided some of the same validation, sense of identity and forum for discussion and questions.

> *John* There are a lot of ex-church Christians who do things socially, meet for coffee, films, breakfast. Do we set up structures, etc.? No, but informally yes.

> *Maree* It's those friendships that keep me going really, and also in a strange way my faith, although my faith has changed, it has been stripped. You have got to have that sounding board, you have got to talk with people. I think it's their experiences that shed light on my own. I've got a couple of friends who I would call quite good thinkers, people who are searching out things, and getting their feedback has been tremendously invaluable. In a way, even though you find things being stripped away, you also find that foundation of faith there. We are getting together because these things are precious to us. It's not something that people do lightly. You don't just leave the church lightly.

The Christian church has always placed an enormous priority on the communal nature of the faith. The church, the *Laos Theou* (People of God), has throughout history seen little room for isolates within the faith and has from the very earliest times highlighted the importance of 'meeting together'. As one church leader I interviewed said, it is a 'relational faith'. It would appear, however, that the Reflective Exiles' need for space, and their tendency to push away from anything that reminds them of the faith package which has failed them, often led them to exit church and not link up with others of like faith.

The post-church groups had one common feature. They had all formed, at least in part, to provide a forum to discuss topics and issues that are not normally up for discussion within EPC churches. In these groups it is possible to admit doubt about faith, failure in faith practices, anger or disappointment at the church or God and to ask essential questions that go to the very core of EPC theology, beliefs and practices. The questions, doubts and emotions that leavers perceive to be out of bounds within EPC churches are celebrated within the post-church groups that they form.

> *Fiona* There are so many issues. How do you forgive somebody? You know, things like that. Issues of authority for women. What is the role of authority in a church? So many issues. What makes you a Christian? Do you have to pray to be a Christian? To bring up these issues even in a house group [*church-based group*] people would look at you in a strange way.

> *Ruth* The group was just to have some other people who would hear your story out and validate you, who knew where you are at. We had ground rules: what you agreed to this week, you didn't have to agree to the next week. And what your opinion is this week no one would hold you to next week.

The freedom to talk about where they were actually at with their faith, and express doubts and questions was a crucial factor common to people from all the groups I have met. This feature has become an underlying and appreciated aspect of the Spirited Exchanges group for people who have left church or are finding themselves on the margins of EPC church life and belief. The Um Group is a good illustration of such a group.

The title, Um Group, is an interesting reflection on the faith understandings, maturity and position of the people who make up this group. It was intended to reflect their lack of certainty on many issues, their preparedness to hold these issues open for critique without necessarily solving them, and their ability to look at the difficult 'grey' issues while not needing to retreat to clear 'black and white' answers. This shows the priority given to 'not knowing' by many church leavers. Yet it is a special kind of 'not knowing'. Ward and Wild in their discussion of women church leavers speak of the 'I don't know' that is paradoxically full of knowledge. The title Um Group reflects both the ethos of the group and this essence of this paradox. Melanie described the nature of the group in saying:

> *Melanie* We don't do worship there. We start by going round and saying what is happening in our lives since we last met. We talk about that, and then we

have one person, decided ahead of time, who takes the role of leader for that particular evening. This person prepares some input, so this part is more like a study group except that we have never ever done any Bible study – it is not a worship or prayer group. We have talked about prayer, and what it means for the Bible to be inspired, but it is not worship. We don't sing and pray together.

The group functions in an open way typical of other groups I have seen. There is, as Melanie says, 'a pact of being able to say anything', a place where people can 'express any degree of doubts or scepticism'. It has developed a non-judgemental ethos which gives the members tremendous freedom to range far and wide in their thoughts and discussion and to explore all manner of issues. For example, the group has talked about dreams, politics and sexuality as well as topics related to their faith.

For those who do become involved in post-church groups, it is not just in order to process faith issues and to continue with faith practices but also for a group of people to belong to. Leavers consistently comment on the loss of a sense of community and a place of belonging that resulted from their decision to leave their church. Involvement in a group to some degree meets this longing to belong and replaces something of their loss of community.

Some groups, like Stuart and Michelle's, were begun by church leavers. Two other groups I am aware of were begun by counsellors or psycho-therapists. The formation of the two groups came about when a trained counsellor who had been working with a number of ex-church clients saw the need for a group where these people could talk and relate together. The counsellors were themselves Christians and were concerned about the pain and struggle of those leaving the church. Again the key focus of these groups was to provide a safe place for people to deal with their grief, loss and anger through the process of leaving the church. In such groups there is the added stability of a skilled person who can both encourage open and honest discussion and reflection on people's faith while at the same time providing something of a model of Christian faith beyond the difficult passages of faith that so many leavers inhabit.

Spirited Exchanges is very much like the two groups begun by Christian counsellors described above. At Spirited Exchanges there is a mix of people who have walked their own journey of EPC faith and church dissolution and subsequent faith rebuilding, and those who come in the midst of their own faith crises and struggles. It is intentionally a safe place where people can express their own doubts, beliefs, experiences and ideas in an environment in which they will be listened to and accepted. People are free to express their emotions and thoughts without fear of others judging or trying to change them.

I have found it helpful to distinguish between two principal orientations in post-church groups: marginal and liminal. By 'marginal' I am referring to the way such groups define themselves in relation to the EPC faith and church structures they have left. 'Liminal' groups, on the other hand, focus on new faith constructions and ways of nurturing and developing faith.

Marginal groups

Ward and Wild state that 'to define oneself as marginal is to define one's self in relation to someone else's centre; it is to accept another's definition of how things are. To have one's base and focus on the margins is to have a view of the present and the past, but what of the future?' (Ward and Wild, 1995, p. 30). Marginal groups tend to focus on what they have left. They are conscious of and give energy and space to the deconstruction of previous beliefs and understandings. They express feelings about their time within EPC churches and their subsequent feelings. In a blunt sense such groups act as old boys' clubs. The uniting feature is a previous common experience which has now passed but is nevertheless significant for their sense of identity.

Liminal groups

The word 'liminal', from the Latin *limen* (threshold), was first used by the anthropologist Arnold van Gennep. The liminal signifies the in-between time. Arnold van Gennep described it as like the neutral zone that often existed between nations in antiquity. He described these zones as often being deserts, marshes or virgin forest where everyone had full rights to travel and hunt. 'Liminality, therefore, can be described as an ambiguous, sacred, social state in which a person or group of persons is separated for a time from the normal structure of society' (van Gennep, 1960, pp. 17–19). It is the threshold of the new. Whereas the marginal group is primarily focused on the past which they have left and is continuing to make sense of their leaving, the liminal group is primarily focused on what lies in the future. In faith terms it is looking to develop, build and nurture an ongoing faith.

The marginal–liminal dichotomy is a simplistic characterization of post-church group life. Inevitably all groups give time and energy to unpacking their previous faith and church involvement and looking to nurture and provide resources for the ongoing faith of group participants. While the dichotomy is therefore overly simplistic, many groups have a primary focus on one or other task. Groups made up of recent church leavers and those contemplating leaving are almost completely focused on what they are leaving and are therefore predominantly marginal in nature. Groups with a core of Disillusioned Followers and Reflective Exiles are typically marginally focused as well. Some groups – often those made up of church leavers who have been outside of church for some time and with strong Transitional Explorers and Integrated Wayfinders – are predominately liminal in focus.

Groups can also shift their primary focus as the centre of gravity in the group members shifts from a greater marginal focus to an increasing liminality.

Bread & Breakfast is primarily a liminally focused group. The group meets every second Sunday morning at nine o'clock for a leisurely breakfast and an opportunity for an informal chat. After breakfast the group moves to the service part which lasts for approximately an hour. The group prepares its own material, writes its own liturgy and is often focused around a time of communion. The gathering is informal and relaxed, yet thoughtful and engaging. Tony and Melanie, who are members of the group, describe it, saying:

Tony We are, in fact, back in church. Bread & Breakfast is a church, but it is a very different model.

Melanie What it does is it enables us to self-reflect in a totally honest and open way.

I stood there, at the group the other Sunday, and counted 20 adults and about 20 kids and I thought *wow*, what a privilege being here. I just felt so energized by being in this group, and at last my hopes about not fighting irrelevant stuff, all that has come to be. The things I put my time into now in terms of this group are just things I love and think are worthwhile. We had some people come, like a friend who I was having lunch with today. She and her husband now come and they have been attending for about six months. I was talking to her today about her spiritual journey and she has really found something, she has the Eucharist and there is something blossoming in there for her, and she would never ever go near a church. She is really a very intelligent vivacious leader sort of type of person. I would never ever take someone like that into a normal church. I mean, I just would be too embarrassed.

Having watched these liminal groups for some time it is my growing conviction that such groups can provide glimpses of new ways of constructing and nurturing Christian faith. Ways that naturally fit many people alienated or disinterested in church, people who are very comfortable in the chaotic and rapidly changing social context that we often call postmodernity. Where the liminal groups have let go of the dead faith, practices and structures of the EPC churches that have to them become oppressive and destructive, we may find indications of ways of doing church that will connect with many in our wider society. If so, such liminal groups are prophetic in their existence and may be able to give invaluable insights to EPC church leaderships about how to 'be church' in a way that connects with a growing number of people immersed in the chaotic and changing realm of postmodernity.

There is much that the EPC church can learn from those in liminally focused groups outside the church structures. But first we need to recognize the validity of these people's Christian faith and experience. As Ward and Wild state:

> Christians who tend to express their faith outside or on the fringes of the institutional churches are not necessarily a bunch of unfaithful doubters whom the churches should tolerate or regard as a pastoral problem. Rather they are Christians called into the wilderness to find new ways of being church, forming faith communities with their own theological and liturgical life and with much to offer the 'mainstream' churches. (Ward and Wild, 1995, p. 3)

A conversation between EPC churches and liminal groups

In this final section I intend proposing a conversation between EPC church leaders and members of liminal post-church groups. It is a conversation that I believe needs to occur in order to strengthen both EPC churches and post-church groups. The churches have much to learn from the gatherings of their ex-members, and post-church groups can still learn from the EPC churches they have left. Although I am well aware of the enormous barriers – particularly from EPC church leaderships – to such a conversation, the potential mutual gains persuade me that this is an extremely important dialogue, one that church leaders can no longer simply ignore.

What if church leaderships could talk with those in liminal post-church groups? What would they learn? Before we move into the specific strengths of the liminal groups we need to remember that this is a two-way conversation and it will be important also to highlight the distinct strengths of the EPC churches from which post-church groups can also learn. My interviews and discussions with church leavers and knowledge of liminal post-church groups leads me to suggest EPC churches could gain much from the following strengths of post-church groups:

LIMINAL GROUPS HAVE AN INHERENT CONNECTION WITH THE EMERGING POSTMODERN CULTURE

Those in liminal groups are often aware of the greater societal rejection of the meta-narrative approach to life. They either consciously or intuitively realize that truth is multidimensional, paradoxical and connected both to its historical and emerging representations. These individuals and groups have a recognition of the truth claims of Scriptures, religious traditions, science, reason and human philosophies. They are comfortable with the aspects of truth they have apprehended and conscious of both their truth system's points of solidity and inherent gaps. They, like a growing proportion of the wider society, reject the notion of an overarching meta-narrative that provides certainty, coherence and completeness. In their search for 'truth to live by' they have broadened their understanding to leave room for the claims of others from divergent faith stances. In this way they are aware of the nature of the journey on the road to truth and the need for dialogue with others who are on similar journeys. In so doing they fit well with Walter Brueggemann's notion of constructing faith through funding the postmodern imagination (Brueggemann, cited in Tomlinson, 1995, p. 82).

The liminal groups are engaged in the task of funding the postmodern imagination, 'to provide the pieces, materials and resources out of which a new world can be imagined. The struggling efforts of these communities . . . have little to do with forging a new grand scheme or coherent systems, but the voicing of a lot of little pieces out of which people can put life together in fresh configurations' (Veling, 1996, p. 103)

These leavers in liminal groups are at home in the joining of the little pieces to form fresh faith configurations. In stating this I am aware of the cries of relativism that will be levelled at them. Yet the Integrated Wayfinders and liminal groups have not rejected Scripture's basis to knowledge. They have incorporated such knowledge on a convictional and personal basis rather than because of external authoritative claims. Liminal groups are often prepared to hold open their faith understandings to the questions of the emerging postmodernist era. This gives them a greater sense of the issues and questions of our society. In this way they are aware of the need to reshape theology for a new cultural context. As McFague states, 'In order to do theology one must in each age do it differently. To refuse this task is to settle for a theology appropriate for some other time than one's own' (quoted in Veling, 1996, p. 57).

LIMINAL GROUPS HAVE GIVEN PRIORITY TO THE QUESTIONS OF A NEW AGE

Those in liminal groups are personally aware of the way experience has tainted the certitude of their previous EPC faith understanding. Whether it be the personal struggles and suffering of life, the intellectual questioning of the bases of the EPC faith, the realization of the discriminative practices of such churches (especially towards women), or the seeming irrelevance of the church concerns to the concerns of a wider society, these leavers are aware that the old certainties they once held to no longer fit. As such, these leavers are aware of the priority of the question, the unceasing question which is brought to the fore by personal suffering and experience. This is the question that must take priority over the sure and quick answer. It is an awareness that 'allows the subject matter to orient the conversation rather than predetermined answers that push too hastily toward closure' (quoted in Veling, 1996, p. 42). Those in liminal groups place a priority on the question that needs to be felt and honoured in all its complexity and intensity prior to and throughout the process of seeking answers. Their perception of EPC churches is of places that jumped too quickly and too surely to the certainties of their own answers without giving due weight to the depth and complexity of questions.

LIMINAL GROUPS HAVE LEARNED FROM THE JOURNEY OF EXILE

The Integrated Wayfinders and many of those in liminal groups have through personal experience come to the point that Paul Ricoeur talked of as 'beyond the desert of criticism, where we wish to be called again' (Ricoeur, 1967, p. 349). That is, the place that seeks to reconstruct a faith out of the pieces of the past and the new understandings drawn from the personal journey into exile. For the Integrated Wayfinders and those in liminal groups this faith has a distinctly Christian focus. Such groups and individuals have much to say to those who deny the place of any deconstruction of the faith within the EPC churches. They know through personal experience that 'there are times when we need to lose our way in order to be brought to a place of lostness, where the question can emerge'. They know that it is 'not this lostness itself that sustains us; rather, it serves to point us in a new direction, to find another way' (Veling, 1996, p. 145).

The point that needs to be made to the leaders within the EPC churches is that there is valid, Christian faith on the other side of the journey of the exiled which does not mean recapitulation to the faith contents and practices of the EPC churches. And that space needs to be made within EPC churches for people's questions, doubts and experiences of life that do not fit neatly into EPC faith doctrines.

LIMINAL GROUPS INDICATE OTHER WAYS OF STRUCTURING CHRISTIAN COMMUNITY THAN THAT TYPICALLY EMPLOYED BY EPC CHURCHES

The liminal groups that I observed and those the interviewees described to me have much in common with the emergent faith groups that Riddell writes about in his models of an emerging church in what he calls the 'Post Christian West'. The structural emphasis that he identifies includes a high priority for relationships, a focus on what is honest and real, a desire for minimal structures, rented rather than owned buildings and maintaining a relatively small size of group. Riddell says, 'They are wary of growing to a size where the relationships which they value so much may be inhibited' (Riddell, 1998). The emergence of such groups with values that contradict so clearly the church growth values espoused by many EPC churches needs to be considered.

Leonardo Boff points to the significance of such groups in any context where individuals are 'swallowed up in the massive structures of macro-organizations and bureaucracies'. Here Boff sees signs of:

> Renewed hope in the growing phenomenon of small Christian communities springing up around the world, communities that are characterised by their desire to reclaim a strong commitment to mutual relationships, inclusive participation, and honest dialogue among equals. This relational character of intentional Christian communities represents a significant counter-movement to the sense of isolation and estrangement typical of twentieth-century life. (Quoted in Veling, 1996, p. 120)

The focus on whole-of-life relationships is evident within the groups I observed. They differ from church-based groups that focus on segmented aspects of people's lives, typically the 'spiritual'. The liminal groups, in contrast, had a more holistic focus on the wider lives of the participants. They are places of laughter and tears.

The emphasis of the liminal groups raises questions regarding the most appropriate structure for Christian communities in an increasingly post-modern society. Does the postmodernist society indicate that smaller, less clearly structured groups with a high priority on relationships, honesty, integrity and reality have greater connection with the emerging society? If this is the case, what does it imply for the agendas of the mega-church models so much in vogue at the time of writing? As Tomlinson says:

> People see in the church just more of what they see *and reject* in the outside world: hierarchies, bureaucracies, and power struggles. And as Drane says, 'They know that this is not what will bring them personal spiritual fulfillment.' This is not a time for churches to be working towards 'bigger', 'better' and 'more powerful'; it is a time for the church to follow the example of its Lord and divest itself of its power, with all the personality jostling, political manoeuvres and empire-building that goes with it – the postmodern world is not impressed! (Tomlinson, 1995, pp. 144–5; italics as cited)

LIMINAL GROUPS HAVE AN OPENNESS TO PEOPLE WHO THINK DIFFERENTLY

A dominant theme among liminal groups was their openness to those of differing faith and ideological viewpoints. This openness is not an outright acceptance of anything and everything. It is not simply a move to relativism, but an openness enabled through deep personal conviction. As Walter Lowe states:

> Openness is a second-level virtue. Often we speak of openness as though it were a primary virtue like faith, hope, love, prudence, or courage. But it is not; it is derivative. When you have only openness you don't have much. A window stuck *open* is as useless as a window stuck *shut*. In either case you have lost the use of the window . . . Openness is possible for persons or communities who know who they are. When the spine of identity is well established, it is possible to risk relating in depth to those who are different from the self. (Quoted in Fowler, 1991, p. 151; italics as cited)

LIMINAL GROUPS HAVE A BROAD ECLECTIC APPROACH TO LITURGY AND WORSHIP

Liminal groups display a willingness to draw liturgical prayer and worship patterns from a wide variety of sources. They tend to cross old theological and denominational boundaries in this search. Examples of the material that is used include liturgical approaches of mainline churches, writings from historical Catholic, Celtic, Taizé or alternative origins, or the production of their own liturgical forms, as in the case of the Bread & Breakfast group. Often there is a new emphasis on symbolism and more contemplative forms of worship. Added to these, a number of groups included in their spiritual quest material from outside the church, such as the use of psycho-drama, courses like the Enneagram, and feminist approaches and understandings. Some also spoke of a greater connection between the everyday aspects of their lives and their faith.

LIMINAL GROUPS POINT TO A DIFFICULT JOURNEY FOR
THE EPC CHURCH

Perhaps one of the greatest lessons that liminal groups have to offer the EPC churches and their leadership is their knowledge of the difficult journey they individually travelled from the centre of an EPC church to the formation of an integrated and communal Christian faith. In so doing they may allay forlorn hopes within EPC churches that they can continue into a postmodern society in a business-as-usual mode. The journeys of the individual leavers tend to indicate that this will not be possible. The long journey of exile from their faith understandings, values and expected behaviours through periods of deconstruction, examination of the taken-for-granteds and eventual reconstruction of the faith components that survived their scrutiny and experience into a new faith construct, cannot be bypassed by either individuals, groups or churches. EPC church leaders need a realization of the extent of dismantling and rebuilding necessary to move the present EPC faith and church structures to a place of connection with a postmodern society. The degree of fundamental change required should not be underestimated.

EPC churches' perspective

If liminal groups raise a number of issues for the EPC churches then the perspective of those within such churches towards the leavers pose questions of similar magnitude. It is to these questions that we will now turn. As the leaders within the EPC churches look at the faith of the leavers and the liminal groups that are emerging, they too have critical issues to raise.

EPC CHURCHES PERCEIVE A PRIORITY TO MISSION

The EPC churches have in their own communities and through connections with world mission agencies been heavily involved in mission. EPC churches are growing rapidly across the globe, especially in the third world. This is due to the concentrated effort of such churches towards world and local mission. Although the word 'mission' carries a number of meanings for church leavers, its priority as an aspect of Christian faith remains undeniable. Yet church leavers and post-church groups can often lose something of this priority. This lack of a priority to mission was a concern for one leader in a world mission organization. When he heard of another group of leavers who were moving out of an EPC church he said: 'Well, that's another group which is lost to the cause of overseas development in mission.'

However, this was not true of all the groups that I studied. At least one had a high priority to local mission, particularly to refugees who were moving into their city. It was, however, a dormant priority in many others. In part, the move away from giving energy to mission may be a reflection of the leaver's attitude to the activism characteristic of EPC churches or a desire to adopt a greater degree of reflectiveness towards their faith. Whatever the reason, EPC churches can help the post-church groups to redefine their understanding of mission and prioritize their own connection to appropriate forms of world mission

EPC CHURCHES PERCEIVE A PRIORITY FOR EVANGELISM AND CONVERSION

Linked to the priority of mission is a priority for one subcategory of mission, that of evangelism. Not surprisingly, in leaving the EPC churches, leavers have stood back from this core priority of the evangelical movement. Alongside this is a suspicion of the role of evangelism and conversion, in favour of the more gradual process of faith development and maturity. While the evangelical movement has focused on evangelism and conversion at the expense of a similar focus on spiritual development[3] and the journeys of faith development, the reverse priority can be seen in many groups of leavers. This is one of the weaknesses of the fifth stage of faith; at this stage people can have a 'subdued sense of the imperative to share and commend the Christian story in evangelization' (Fowler, 1987, p. 95).

Fowler's work on faith development describes what he calls 'the dual movements of conversion and development' as being both separate and necessary ingredients of the dance of faith (Fowler, 1987, p. 94). Here the leavers, the groups they form and the EPC churches can act as a necessary counterbalance to each other's priorities. This is an area where it is too easy to simply throw out the baby with the bath water. While some approaches and forms of evangelism may be increasingly questioned, the place of evangelism and conversion in the Christian faith cannot simply be ignored.

EPC CHURCHES PERCEIVE THE NEED FOR INVESTMENT IN THE FAITH OF THE NEXT GENERATION

The mission leader quoted above also commented on the groups of leavers he had met that had little energy for supporting the faith of those younger than themselves.

> *Mission leader* The biggest danger area of people dropping out of faith is that they leave before they hit that stage of feeling responsible for the next generation. It's in the thirty to forty age group where our individualism is still there enough for them to say, 'The church is not meeting my needs.' They haven't grown into the maturity to see that they've got to put something back into it, so they drop out. Drop out permanently.

Here the mission leader highlights a weakness of many of the groups set up by leavers. Such groups are geared to cater for people grappling with the same issues regarding church and engaged in similar faith transitions. In so doing, these groups are unaware of the degree to which they alienate people from differing faith stages. This would also be true of the children of many of those interviewed. Such groups focus on the issues at one point of the faith journey, which has led to less of a priority being given to the faith development, education and nurture of their own children's faith as well as that of other people with whom they are in contact.

Coupled with this there is a tendency for people involved in difficult faith transitions to foist their questions and difficulties into contexts in which they only serve to destabilize the faith of others who are not themselves facing similar issues. Those within EPC churches may be right in asserting that such groups will not attract many teenagers, young adults and those outside the Christian faith, at least if they continue in their present form.

EPC CHURCHES PERCEIVE A NEED OF SOMEWHERE TO BELONG

The exilic experience is essentially an experience of homelessness, a homelessness which links with the disturbing absence of meaning and the sense of being isolated which is prevalent in the modern age.

While there is a sense that to really belong to a tradition one must leave that same tradition and stand outside of it, yet one must also return, at least to some degree, to fully belong. Sadly, many leavers are effectively becoming the perpetually homeless. This isolation of faith stands in sharp contrast to the essence of Christian faith described as the *Laos Theou* – the people of God. The Christian faith has throughout history endorsed the communal nature of its being.

Those within the EPC churches can point to the leaver's need for continued community. What is needed is a sense of belonging – a place, community or people with which to belong.

EPC CHURCHES HAVE A PREPAREDNESS TO LEARN FROM THE CLASSICS OF THE FAITH

Many of the post-church groups that were observed as part of this study allow little space for the classic writings of the Christian faith, perhaps especially the Scriptures. In their wilderness phase people characteristically give up reading the Bible and other Christian texts and tend to turn to other sources. The groups developed among leavers can often continue this reluctance in terms of the Christian tradition, Scriptures and classics. Because such groups usually involve a number of people who may be at different places in their own faith journeys, there is a tendency for the programme of the groups to be swayed by those reluctant to incorporate Scripture and Christian tradition. While this is a natural part of the deconstruction of faith and the incorporation of a broader faith understanding, some priority needs to be given to the Scriptures and Christian classics for people's ongoing inspiration and guidance in faith.

EPC CHURCHES PERCEIVE THE NEED TO MAINTAIN CONNECTIONS WITH OTHER LARGER CONGLOMERATIONS OF PEOPLE

Part of the strength of the evangelical spectrum of the church has been its ability to cross denominational boundaries in order to bring together resources for the sake of larger projects. These projects have included working across denominational and church boundaries to establish theological and mission training centers and media groups like the Christian radio stations.

While liminal groups and EPC leavers may not want to build the same type of institutions, there is nevertheless strength in networks and larger conglomerations into which people and groups are connected. The Internet appears to be a means through which this is beginning to happen, as *The Prodigal Project* has illustrated. While the book *The Prodigal Project* was written by Mike Riddell, Mark Pierson and Cathy Kirkpatrick (2000), the CD has music, images, video, photographs and artwork by dozens of people worldwide as well as a series of Internet connections. In its use of these media and networking, *The Prodigal Project* is a product of a whole emerging form of church.

EPC CHURCHES PERCEIVE THE NEED FOR ENERGY AND RISK TAKING IN THE NAME OF FAITH

Fowler writes of the weaknesses of the fifth stage of faith, saying there 'can be a sense of paralysis and retreat into a private world of spirituality'. This sense of immobility can 'if prolonged, lead to a cutting of the call to partnership with God' (Fowler, 1987, p. 95). By the term 'partnership with God', Fowler is referring to the involvement in the work of God in the world. This is a weakness that isolated church leavers can easily fall into.

Hope of an ongoing dialogue

Having discussed some specific areas in which the liminal groups (developed by EPC church leavers) have valid criticisms of the EPC church they have left, as well as the equally valid criticisms by leaders within EPC churches, I want to conclude by pleading for open channels of communication between church leaderships and people who are considering leaving and between church leavers and church leaderships. There is much to gain from each other's experience of Christian faith and the strengths of the different expressions of faith. Without such a discussion I fear for the robustness of the Christian faith in our increasingly post-Christian and postmodern age.

If EPC churches and post-church groups can establish meaningful dialogue and share what they have gained from their respective faith journeys, then increasingly robust and culturally relevant communities of Christian faith may result. It's my prayer that those inside the church and those outside can create circles which include each other rather than cut each other out.

NOTES

1 Edwin Markham, 'Outwitted', *Epigrams*, 1901.
2 The use of the hyphen in this way is drawn from John Drane (2000, p. 6) who makes a similar use of a hyphen in the term 'postmodern'.
3 Alister McGrath, for example, states: 'My concern is that evangelicals have not paid anything like the necessary attention to this major theme *spiritual development* of Christian life and thought. As a result, evangelicalism has become impoverished' (McGrath, 1994, p. 125; italics mine).

Bibliography

Anderson, D., 1995. 'Disquiet in the Tornado', *Canadian Baptist*, March, pp. 7–8.

Barrett, D. B. (ed.), 1982. *World Christian Encyclopaedia: A Comparative Study of Churches and Religions in the Modern World,* A D 1900–2000, Nairobi, Kenya, Oxford University Press.

Barrett, D. B., 1988. 'The Twentieth-Century Pentecostal/Charismatic Renewal in the Holy Spirit, with its Goal of World Evangelization', *International Bulletin of Missionary Research*, July, pp. 119–29.

Barrett, D. B., 1997. 'Annual Statistical Table on Global Mission: 1997', *International Bulletin of Missionary Research*, January, pp. 24–5.

Bauman, Z., 1992. *Intimations of Postmodernity*, London, Routledge.

Bauman, Z., 1997. *Postmodernity and its Discontents*, Oxford and Cambridge, Polity Press.

Bebbington, D. W., 1989. *Evangelicalism in Modern Britain: A History from the 1730s to the 1980s*, London, Unwin Hyman.

Brierley, P., 2000. *The Tide is Running Out: What the English Church Attendance Survey Tells Us*, London, Christian Research.

Brinkerhoff, M. B. and Burke, K. L., 1980. 'Disaffiliation: Some Notes on "Falling from Faith"', *Sociological Analysis*, vol. 41, no. 1, pp. 41–5.

Bromley, D. G. (ed.), 1988. *Falling from the Faith: Causes and Consequences of Religious Apostasy*, Newbury Park, California, Sage Publications, p. 81.

Brueggemann, W., 1991. 'Rethinking Church Models Through Scripture', *Theology Today*, vol. XLVIII, no. 2, July.

Cohen, S. and Taylor, L., 1992. *Escape Attempts*. London, Routledge & Kegan Paul.

Croucher, R. J., 1986. *Recent Trends Among Evangelicals: Biblical Agendas, Justice and Spirituality*, Heathmont, Victoria, John Mark Ministries.

Croucher, R. J., *Why Clergy Leave Parish Ministry*, Melbourne, John Mark Ministries (undated unpublished paper).

Davie, G., 1990. 'Believing without Belonging: Is This the Future of Religion in Britain?' *Social Compass*, vol. 37, pp. 455–69.

Davie, G., 1994. *Religion in Britain since 1945: Believing without Belonging*, Oxford, Blackwell.

Dawn, M., 1997. 'You Have to Change to Stay the Same' in G. Cray *et al.*, *The Post-Evangelical Debate*, London, Triangle, pp. 35–56.

Drane, J., 2000. *The McDonaldization of the Church: Spirituality, Creativity and the Future of the Church*, London, Darton, Longman & Todd.

Ebaugh, H. R. F., 1977. *Out of the Cloister: A Study of Organizational Dilemmas*, Austin, University of Texas Press.

Ebaugh, H. R. F., 1984. 'Leaving the Convent: The Experience of Role Exit and Self-Transformation', in J. A. Kotarba and A. Fontana (eds), *The Existential Self in Society*, Chicago, University of Chicago Press, pp. 156–76.

Ebaugh, H. R. F., 1988. *Becoming an EX: The Process of Role Exit*, Chicago, University of Chicago Press.

Fanstone, M. J., 1993. *The Sheep that Got Away: Why Do People Leave the Church?* Tunbridge Wells, MARC.

Fowler, J. W., 1984. *Becoming Adult, Becoming Christian: Adult Development and Christian Faith*, San Francisco, Harper & Row.

Fowler, J. W., 1987. *Faith Development and Pastoral Care*, Philadelphia, Fortress Press.

Fowler, J. W., 1991. *Weaving the New Creation: Stages of Faith and the Public Church*, San Francisco, HarperCollins.

Fowler, J. W., 1995. *Stages of Faith: The Psychology of Human Development and the Quest for Meaning*, San Francisco, Harper.

Fowler, J. W., 1996. *Faithful Change: The Personal and Public Challenges of Postmodern Life*, Nashville, Abingdon Press.

Fowler, J. W. and Keen, S., 1985. *Life Maps: Conversations on the Journey of Faith*, Waco, Texas, Word Books.

Giddens, A., 1990. *The Consequences of Modernity*, Oxford and Cambridge, Polity Press.

Giddens, A., 1991. *Modernity and Self-Identity: Self and Society in the Late Modern Age*, Oxford and Cambridge, Polity Press.

Gilligan, C., 1982. *In a Different Voice: Psychological Theory and Women's Development*, Cambridge, Massachusetts, Harvard University Press.

Gilling, B., 1992. 'Introduction', in B. Gilling (ed.), *'Be Ye Separate': Fundamentalism and the New Zealand Experience*, Hamilton, New Zealand, University of Waikato and Colcom Press, pp. xi–xv.

Gilling, M., 1999. *Where do We Find Our Meaning?* Auckland, Futures Group of the Methodist Church of New Zealand.

Grainger, R., 1993. *Change to Life*, London, Darton, Longman & Todd.

Hagberg, J. O. and Guelich, R. A., 1989. *The Critical Journey: Stages in the Life of Faith*, Dallas, Word Publishing.

Hendricks, W. D., 1993. *Exit Interviews: Revealing Stories of Why People are Leaving the Church*, Chicago, Moody Press.

Hoge, D. R, Johnson, B. and Luidens, D. A., 1993. 'Determinants of Church Involvement of Young Adults Who Grew Up in Presbyterian Churches', *Journal for the Scientific Study of Religion*, vol. 32, no. 3, pp. 242–55.

Houston, J., 1989. *Prayer the Transforming Friendship: A Guide to the Spiritual Life*, Oxford, Lion.

Hurnard, H., 1993. *Hinds' Feet on High Places*, Illinois, Living Books.

Lyon, D., 2000. *Jesus in Disneyland: Religion in Post-Modern Times*, Oxford and Cambridge, Polity Press.

McCullough, C., 1983. *Heads of Heaven; Feet of Clay*, New York, Pilgrim Press.

McGavran, D., 1955. *The Bridges of God*, New York, Friendship Press.

McGavran, D., 1970. *Understanding Church Growth*, Grand Rapids, Eerdmans.

McGavran, D., 1986. 'My Pilgrimage in Mission', *International Bulletin of Missionary Research*, April, pp. 53–8.

McGrath, A. E., 1994. *Evangelicalism and the Future of Christianity*, London, Hodder & Stoughton.

Mead, L. B., 1993. *The Once and Future Church: Reinventing the Congregation for a New Mission Frontier*, New York, Alban Institute Publication.

Parks, S., 1986. *The Critical Years: The Young Adults Search for a Faith to Live By*, San Francisco, Harper & Row.

Peck, M. S., 1993. *Further Along the Road Less Travelled: The Unending Journey Toward Spiritual Growth*, New York, Simon & Schuster.

Pressau, J. R., 1977. *I'm Saved, You're Saved – Maybe*, Atlanta, John Knox Press.

Richter, P. and Francis, L. J., 1998. *Gone but Not Forgotten: Church Leaving and Returning*, London, Darton, Longman & Todd.

Ricoeur, P., 1967. *The Symbolism of Evil*, Boston, Beacon.

Riddell, M., 1998. *Threshold of the Future: Reforming the Church in the Post-Christian West*, London, SPCK.

Riddell, M., Pierson, M. and Kirkpatrick, C., 2000. *The Prodigal Project*, London, SPCK.

Roof, W. C., 1993. *A Generation of Seekers: The Spiritual Journeys of the Baby Boom Generation*, San Francisco, Harper.

Stokes, K., 1992. *Faith is a Verb: Dynamics of Adult Faith Development*, Mystic, Connecticut, Twenty-third Publications.

Synan, V., 1992. *The Spirit Said 'Grow': The Astounding Worldwide Expansion of Pentecostal and Charismatic Churches*, Monrovia, California, MARC.

Tomlinson, D., 1995. *The Post-Evangelical*, London, Triangle.

Van Gennep, A., 1960. *The Rites of Passage*, Chicago, University of Chicago Press.

Veling, T. A., 1996. *Living in the Margins: Intentional Communities and the Art of Interpretation*, New York, Crossroad.

Wagner, C. P., 1976. *Your Church Can Grow: Seven Vital Signs of a Healthy Church*, Glendale, California, G/L Publications.

Wagner, C. P., 1992. 'Foreword' in V. Synan, *The Spirit Said 'Grow': The Astounding Worldwide Expansion of Pentecostal and Charismatic Churches*, Monrovia, California, MARC.

Ward, H. and Wild, J., 1995. *Guard the Chaos: Finding Meaning in Change*, London, Darton, Longman & Todd.

Index

agnostic 87, 89
alternative faith, transition to 85–9
angry leavers 50–2
autonomous faith 100–2

backsliding 42, 43, 107, 130, 148
Barrett, David 24
Bebbington, David W. 23, 108
Bible, the 16, 24, 49, 53, 55, 57, 61, 63, 64, 65, 66, 68, 70, 72, 86, 87, 91, 92, 93, 94, 114, 156, 169
Boff, Leonardo 164
bold faith 55
Bonhoeffer, Dietrich 120
Brierley, Peter 8
Brinkerhoff, M. B. and Burke, K. L. 8
Bromley, D. G. 8
Brueggemann, Walter 162
Bunyan, John 108

charismatic movement 11, 22, 24, 25, 27
childhood involvement 51
children 1–4, 12–14, 30, 31, 35, 38, 46, 50, 51, 60, 87, 96, 97, 101, 112, 113, 114, 130, 134, 142, 144, 168
church growth movement 27
counter-dependency 66, 67, 73, 80
counter-dependent relationship 66

deconstruction of faith 68, 70, 71, 73, 77, 89, 166
demographics of interviewees 12
dependent relationship 52
Disillusioned Followers 46–59, 61, 62, 63, 66, 94, 102, 154, 155, 159
disillusionment 33, 37, 42, 44, 48, 49, 50
doubting phase 33, 35, 146

Ebaugh, Helen 32, 33–7, 39, 41
emerging self-ownership 84
EPC churches 22
evangelical movement 22, 24, 27, 108, 167
evangelicalism 22–6, 54, 148
exile 43, 65

Fanstone, Michael 8
financial giving 53, 66
Fowler, James 108–25, 126, 147, 148, 168, 170
full-time Christian work 14
full-time study 14
fundamentalism 22–5

Gilling, B. 24

Hendricks, William 8
Hagberg, J. O. and Guelich, R. A. 135, 136, 137
hesitant faith 73

Holmes, Oliver Wendell 138
homosexuality 37, 83
Hurnard, Hannah 108, 151
hurt leavers 50

'I don't know' 56, 61, 64, 70–3, 88,
    146, 156
inner spirituality 131
inner-dependency 80–2, 89, 96
integrated faith 74, 94, 98–100, 103
Integrated Wayfinders 91–105, 154,
    155, 159, 162, 163,
interdependent faith 96–8
interviewing 10

Jesus movement 19–21, 25
Job 99, 101, 134, 135, 137, 138, 139

King, Martin Luther 120
knockbacks 41

leadership
  autocratic 32
  patterns of 25
  positions 13–15, 42, 48
  roles 2, 5, 13, 15, 19, 143, 150
leaving process 29, 31–6, 38, 42, 44,
    63, 150
liberal church 31, 87
liberalism 22
liminal groups 158, 160, 161–6
Lowe, Walter 165

marginal groups 158
Markham, Edwin 152
McCullough, Charles 112
McGavran, Donald 26

McGrath, A. E. 22, 23
mega-churches 26, 165
meta-narrative 61, 161
meta-grumbles 61
mission 167
Mother Teresa 120
mutual withdrawal 41

New Age 85, 89, 162

ongoing reflection 69–72

para-church groups 26
Parks, Sharon 67, 81, 82, 112
Peck, M. Scott 114, 147
Pentecostal movement 25, 27
Pentecostalism 24
post-church groups 16, 153–5, 157–
    61, 169, 171
postmodern culture 6, 9, 122, 161
postmodern society 164, 166
prayer 13, 14, 25, 35, 41, 46, 48, 53,
    56, 61, 65, 66, 68, 72, 86, 87, 93,
    97, 102, 115, 132, 145, 148, 156,
    171

questioning 10, 29, 30, 32, 61, 62, 63,
    67, 69, 70, 80, 84, 92, 94, 95,
    102, 137, 146, 162, 163

received faith 51, 69, 77
reconstruction of faith 82, 83, 89
Reflective Exiles 60–74, 79, 80, 83, 84,
    88, 92, 95, 127, 153, 154, 155, 159
research project 6
returning to church 57
Richter, P. and Francis, L. J. 8, 41, 111
Ricoeur, Paul 137, 163

Riddell, Mike 164, 170

secularization 15
seeker-sensitive services 27, 145
seeking alternatives 35
service to others 53, 66
specific grumbles 50, 54, 56, 62
Spirited Exchanges 7, 109, 142, 145, 156, 157
spiritual direction 131, 148
St John of the Cross 108, 136, 147
St Teresa of Avila 108, 147
St Thomas Aquinas 108
stages of faith 108–21
strengthening faith 84
strong faith 102
Sunday school 12, 13, 19

taken-for-granteds 51, 54, 62, 67, 166
theological study 76, 102, 148
therapy 4
threshold groups 159
Tomlinson, D. 9, 165
Toronto Blessing 46, 48

Transitional Explorers 75–90, 92, 94, 95, 154, 155, 159,
turning point 33, 39, 42, 75

unexamined faith 54

van Gennep, Arnold 158
Veling, T. A. 65, 162, 163

Wagner, C. P. 11
wall, the 135, 137, 139, 143, 147
Ward, H. and Wild, J. 66, 72, 156, 158, 160
Wayfinder 95
what pastors said 40
Wilkerson, David 3
willed naïveté 138
Willow Creek Community Church 27
worship 2, 13, 14, 22, 25, 27, 34, 35, 47, 53, 66, 99, 115, 120, 121, 122, 129, 141, 142, 149, 156, 165

youth group 3, 12, 13, 35, 75, 85, 96

The Society for Promoting Christian Knowledge (SPCK) was founded in 1698. Its mission statement is:

To promote Christian knowledge by

- **Communicating the Christian faith in its rich diversity**
- **Helping people to understand the Christian faith and to develop their personal faith; and**
- **Equipping Christians for mission and ministry**

SPCK Worldwide serves the Church through Christian literature and communication projects in 100 countries, and provides books for those training for ministry in many parts of the developing world. This worldwide service depends upon the generosity of others and all gifts are spent wholly on ministry programmes, without deductions.

SPCK Bookshops support the life of the Christian community by making available a full range of Christian literature and other resources, providing support for those training for ministry, and assisting bookstalls and book agents throughout the UK.

SPCK Publishing produces Christian books and resources, covering a wide range of inspirational, pastoral, practical and academic subjects. Authors are drawn from many different Christian traditions, and publications aim to meet the needs of a wide variety of readers in the UK and throughout the world.

The Society does not necessarily endorse the individual views contained in its publications, but hopes they stimulate readers to think about and further develop their Christian faith.

For information about the Society, visit our website at *www.spck.org.uk*, or write to:
SPCK, Holy Trinity Church, Marylebone Road,
London NW1 4DU, United Kingdom.